AWES

'One of the great g   s,
both male and   ... .SOME *voices* brings
together the lives and stories of some of the hugely
talented women who are now serving God in the
Church of England ministry. Read it and rejoice!'
**Pete Broadbent, Bishop of Willesden and Deputy
Bishop of London**

'Ordained ministry comes in many shapes and forms.
This is an inspiring book of personal stories from
women who are flourishing in the work to which God
has called them. Don't give in to the stereotypes; let
this book be a surprise and encouragement.'
Jackie Searle, Archdeacon of Gloucester

'AWESOME plays a vital role in supporting and
encouraging younger women in ministry. There are
real life stories here of God working in people's lives
and people called to God's service. They will make you
think, help you explore further and inspire you to
faith and action.'
**Steven Croft, Bishop of Sheffield and Chair of the
Ministry Council of the Church of England**

AWESOME VOICES:

God working through

ordained women today

God's strength made perfect in weakness

Gilead Books Publishing
Corner Farm
West Knapton
Malton
North Yorkshire, YO17 8JB, UK
First published in Great Britain, November 2013
2 4 6 8 10 9 7 5 3 1

Copyright © the contributors 2013

British Library Cataloguing-in-Publication Data:
A catalogue record for this book is available from the British Library.

ISBN-13: 978-0-9926713-0-3

All rights reserved.
No part of this publication may be reproduced, stored in a retrieval
system or transmitted in any form or by any means, electronic,
mechanical, photocopying, recording or otherwise, without the prior
permission of the publisher.

All scripture quotations, unless otherwise indicated, are taken from
the HOLY BIBLE, NEW INTERNATIONAL VERSION. Copyright © 1973,
1978, 1984 by International Bible Society. Used by permission of
Hodder & Stoughton, a member of the Hodder Headline Group. All
rights reserved. 'NIV' is a trademark of International Bible Society. UK
trademark number 1448790.

Scripture quotations marked (NRSV) are from the New Revised
Standard Version Bible, copyright © 1989 the Division of Christian
Education of the National Council of the Churches of Christ in the
United States of America. Used by permission. All rights reserved.

Scripture quotations marked (MSG) are taken from The Message.
Copyright © 1993, 1994, 1995, 1996, 2000, 2001, 2002. Used by
permission of NavPress Publishing Group

The publisher makes every effort to ensure that the papers used in
our books are made from trees that have been legally sourced from
well-managed and credibly certified forests by using a printer
awarded FSC & PEFC chain of custody certification.

Cover design: Nathan Ward

Contents

Foreword

It is a great honour to be asked to write a foreword to *AWESOME Voices*.

One of the privileges of the last six years at Birkenhead has been to see the Lord bless awesome women who are benefactors, giving their necks for the lives of others, working hard, beloved, working hard in the Lord; in other words seeing the working out of the ministries of those spoken of in Romans 16 in the Church of England now; apostles, prophets, evangelists, pastors and teachers. I think of one who challenged a rural group of parishes at her interview with "the gospel grows churches", a new idea for them. They wanted her to come but she turned them down (rightly, and they ended up with a gospel man) and she is growing another church with the gospel in another place, the right one for her.

These testimonies are all reasons for similar thanks giving. I hope they will encourage all of us women and men in the ministry to which we have been called and lead us to give the kind of praise with which Romans 16 ends,

> *"Now to God who is able to strengthen you according to my gospel and the proclamation of Jesus Christ, according to the revelation of the*

mystery that was kept secret for long ages but is now disclosed, and through the prophetic writings is made known to all the Gentiles, according to the command of the eternal God, to bring about the obedience of faith—to the only wise God, through Jesus Christ, to whom be the glory forever! Amen" Romans 16:25-27 (NRSV)

Lord raise up more women (and men) for this awesome ministry.

Keith Sinclair
Bishop of Birkenhead

The Authors

Lis Goddard
Chair of AWESOME, Vicar of St James the Less Pimlico, writer and former theological lecturer at Wycliffe Hall Oxford

Jane Plackett & Suse McBay
Jane is an ordinand at St John's College Nottingham, as is Suse who is also studying for a PhD in biblical studies

Sally Hitchiner
Senior Chaplain and Interfaith Advisor at Brunel University, writer and broadcaster

Clare Hendry
Permanent deacon, writer and former lecturer at Oak Hill Theological College, Assistant Minister Grace Church Muswell Hill and Assistant lecturer at Wycliffe Hall Oxford

Jane Morris
Vicar of St Gabriel's Cricklewood and member of the General Synod

Liz Hoare
Writer, Tutor in Spiritual Formation and Dean for Women at Wycliffe Hall Oxford

Kate Wharton
Priest in Charge of St George's Everton

AWESOME finds a voice

Lis Goddard

There are times in our lives, in our ministries, when God takes over. Clearly that is, or should, always be the case, but by this I mean that there are times when God takes control so powerfully and changes our direction so completely in a way which will affect the rest of our life and ministry so fundamentally that it leaves us speechless.

For me NEAC4 (the Fourth National Evangelical Anglican Congress) was just such a time. I knew that it would be difficult in all sorts of ways. Evangelicals were pretty divided. NEACs had traditionally happened every ten years and this had taken fifteen to organise. All those who thought about it knew that this was partly due to the division caused amongst evangelicals by the ordination of women to the priesthood/presbyterate. There was much debate in the run-up to the Congress about the emphases and it took a lot of work to agree to include not just the cross and scripture (with concerns being to hold onto traditional evangelical hermeneutics rather than moving towards the new perspective) but also mission as a third strand, it was symptomatic of the internal battles being fought. Relationships were not easy between so-called conservative/classic and open evangelicals. Rowan Williams had been Archbishop of Canterbury for under a year, during which time there had been the Reading crisis. Rowan had been invited to address NEAC but there was an organised campaign to disinvite him. Alongside that the fallout of the Reading crisis was still very much in everyone's minds, sharpened by the recent election of Gene Robinson to be Bishop of New Hampshire in what was then ECUSA (The Episcopal Church (USA)). It seemed clear that it would be these issues which would dominate proceedings.

It is now ten years since NEAC4 in Blackpool. It will be remembered for many things, but one of the key things could not have been anticipated as we travelled up to Blackpool. Just under ten years on from the ordination of the first women as priests/presbyters in Bristol, Blackpool saw the bringing together of not only thousands of evangelicals lay and ordained but also, for the first time in our history, a significant number of ordained evangelical women. The majority didn't know each other, because the numbers were still small and far flung. There was therefore a feeling of isolation and of being unusual, somehow different, odd and unwelcome, both within the constituency and the church at large. Within the strange context of NEAC the pain and alienation of evangelical women became obvious. Unintentionally NEAC4 had enabled the articulation of something which had up until then been hidden and unspoken.

In the planning of the Congress the organisers had side-lined ordained women. There were very few speaking from the Main Stage—just one deacon from Brazil and Sue Hope from Sheffield Diocese speaking on evangelism. There were more in forums and seminars, and only one contributed to the NEAC book 'Fanning the Flame'. At the Communion Service on the Sunday only three ordained women were involved in the distribution of the elements. The feelings this evoked were powerful—the pain was palpable. It would be unfair to the organisers of the Congress to suggest that all of this was done deliberately. Perhaps it was more indicative of the sort of evangelical churches they came from that they did not know of any ordained evangelical women who could speak in such a context, and therefore assured us that there were none.

Several ordained women found themselves talking—initially in one of the ladies toilets—and the conversation spread. It became clear that this was symptomatic of a wider malaise, of women who had come to faith, who had been nurtured and grown within the evangelical constituency and who had discovered a vocation to ordained ministry, been trained, usually in evangelical colleges and then found that their own constituency no longer recognised or wanted them. Women who felt that they no longer had a home. They felt and were clearly evangelical in their theology and their praxis, so they did not fit comfortably within the broad middle ground or liberal catholic wing of the church. Yet they were told that by definition, because of their gender and calling, they could not be fully evangelical. There were dreadful stories of women being slow-handclapped by male colleagues, of female curates or associate vicars being marginalised. Alternatively, evangelical women just could not find jobs in evangelical churches and found themselves going to jobs outside their churchmanship. This in itself is not a bad thing but it was taken by some of the evangelical constituency as proof that, as they suspected, the women were indeed not really evangelical. Men were getting the evangelical jobs, men were allowed to speak at evangelical gatherings (as were, interestingly, lay women and those married to male leaders). In contrast, the ordained women were regularly made to feel that, just because they were ordained, just because they wore a dog-collar, they could not, by definition, be truly evangelical. They could not, by definition, take the Bible seriously.

Of course for evangelicals this was a tricky issue because there was a whole cohort for whom women teaching or being in leadership is unacceptable on biblical and theological grounds, but this was certainly not the case across the board. One of the key problems was that even in some places where women's ordination should have been encouraged this was not always the case. There were examples of good practice, of places where women were welcomed and nurtured, but it became quickly clear that evangelical women felt marginalised, voiceless and unsupported.

I was given 3 minutes on the Main Stage to encourage all the ordained women at the conference to gather together before NEAC dispersed—so that we could get together and see where God took us. I spoke about how important it was that as evangelicals we should work together and not against each other, learning to trust each other rather than assuming the worst, and I asked that we be given a chance to move forward together—all evangelicals—for the sake of the gospel and the kingdom. I was overwhelmed by the response. I and a couple of others gathered names and email addresses after the session and then Susie Sanders, Bonnie Appleton and I started planning our first conference.

We had an interim name: WEAC (Women Evangelical Anglican Clergy). We set up a baby website and I wrote a piece for the Church of England Newspaper (CEN) encouraging other women to join us—either at the conference in January 2004 or via the website. We set out our aims as agreed in the corner of the Great Hall at NEAC4 in Blackpool—"To support and equip one another for ordained ministry...that the Church might be better equipped to fulfil her gospel imperative". We sought to gather evangelical ordained women within the Church of England praying for one another and supporting one another across the evangelical spectrum—all evangelical ordained women across the whole evangelical spectrum. This meant that we deliberately set out to include all three orders from the beginning—clearly that initially meant and currently still means just deacons—permanent or otherwise—and priests/presbyters—but we were always clear that it would also, in God's good time—and Synod's—include bishops. The breadth of the group inevitably meant that not all of us were, or indeed are, in favour either of women ordained to the priesthood or the episcopate. We decided however that the key thing was to work together as evangelical women, supporting each other.

At that first conference, which met at Wycliffe Hall on 8 January 2004, 28 women came together to worship, and to put the building blocks in place. We changed our name—partly because we felt that WEAC gave the wrong impression and also because there is a group of clergy wives who use that acronym. After much discussion we agreed on AWESOME. This was not, as many have supposed, a triumphalist reflection on how we view ourselves but more a reflection on the God we serve and His work in and through us. It also worked as an acronym: Anglican Women Evangelicals: Supporting our Ordained Ministries. The acronym has always been defined by the strapline from 2 Corinthians 12:9 "God's strength made perfect in weakness". We have always been aware that we start from a position of weakness, not because we are women, but because "...we have this treasure in jars of clay, to show that this all surpassing power is from God and not from us" (2 Corinthians 4:7). We started from a position of extreme weakness and felt hard-pressed on every side, but we have always been clear that it has been about God and not us. He is indeed Awesome.

Alongside that we also agreed on aims and elected our first committee. Our aims were to be clear. We were not going to be another political, campaigning group – there were groups doing that and besides we had different views on the main presenting issue of women bishops. That did not mean that we would not in practice talk about it, just that we would do it in a different way. Our aims would be the support of evangelical women ordained within the Church of England, equipping them for full inclusion within the church as a whole and the evangelical wing in particular. With this in mind we would work towards supporting evangelical women in all their giftings. We would establish area networks which would be safe spaces for encouragement, sharing and prayer. We would enable and equip for mentoring. We would actively work for ordained women speakers at large events, raising their profile and promoting the skills of preaching, teaching and public speaking. Aware of how key theological education was, we would also encourage and raise the profile of women as theological educators. We would do our best to enable and promote the appointment of evangelical women to evangelical posts, working with patronage boards and those with the power to appoint to encourage them to see potential rather than to assume that they need to accept the status quo. And within all of this we would work hard to ensure that the gospel and scripture remained absolutely central.

A later committee summarised it as follows:

> *To be a voice for evangelical women*
> *To encourage women to grow in their vocations*
> *To support each other in ministry through networks and mentoring*
> *To raise the profile of women at local and national level*
> *To engage with practical biblical and theological issues*
> *"We exist to support and pray for one another in ministry, learning from scripture, the Spirit and one another. We seek to equip one another for ordained ministry in the Church, that the Church might be better equipped to fulfil her gospel imperative."*

It was agreed that we would adopt the CEEC statement of faith as holding together what we wanted to say about ourselves.

And so AWESOME began.

I found myself elected as Chair (I was then Chaplain of Jesus College, Oxford and later that year moved to be Tutor for Ministerial Formation at Wycliffe Hall, Oxford) with two vice-Chairs Susie Sanders (Vicar of Christ Church and St Martha on the Hill Guildford) and Bonnie Appleton (Diocesan Missioner to Guildford Diocese). In addition to this we agreed that there should always be a Permanent Deacons rep so Clare Hendry (Tutor for Pastoral Counselling at Oak Hill College) joined us to represent that group. Then we had Lucy Holt (curate of Newton Longville and Mursley) as Treasurer and Secretary, Tamsin Merchant (curate at St John's Harborne) as Web and publicity co-ordinator; Katie Tupling (curate at St Peter's Belper) as Regional group/Network co-ordinator.

We were a small group then and felt pretty much ignored and inconsequential. It took a long time for things to begin to happen and to change but there is little doubt that over the last ten years a lot has changed and we have seen God work in remarkable ways. If you had asked me in 2003 I would never have expected to be involved in or to have achieved all that we have done over that past 10 years. There is no doubt that the movement of the Spirit which began AWESOME has changed my life and ministry and that of others significantly. It would be impossible to write about it all but I think it is important to outline the highlights.

Perhaps one of the most significant things which have happened is our regular conferences. These have become vital times for evangelical women to come away from their ministry contexts and to be refreshed; to take time out and to be equipped and restored for the journey. I have lost count of the number of times that I have heard women say "I don't usually 'do' women's events but this is different, thank you". We have covered everything from mission (Sue Hope) to retreat and spirituality (Anne Dyer), from restoring order into the busy-ness (Elaine Storkey/Emma Ineson) to preaching (Erin Clifford), from dealing with conflict (Rachel Treweek) to discipleship (Jane Morris), and realising God-given potential (Jackie Searle) all earthed firmly in scripture and worship. We have given women time to rest, to meet other women in similar contexts, to compare notes, to talk freely about their struggles and their excitements and to be pampered. We know that there are women for whom these conferences are important markers in their yearly or bi-annual calendar.

Alongside the conferences, which bring people together from across the country, there is also the local expression of AWESOME—the Local Networks. These take different expressions in each locality, some choosing to meet together over a meal for fellowship and prayer support and others choosing to be intentional and to have a clear learning purpose to their meeting. The number of Networks has fluctuated and their make-up varied according to clergy moves, but they have steadily grown and we now have most of the country covered—apart from the North-East. They have become an important way of ensuring that evangelical ordained women are not isolated and that, in contrast with 2003, in any given region there is a good chance that they will know each other and be able to provide real support. They offer a context where evangelical women can discuss openly and freely how it feels and what is happening. There is no other context where this can happen in the same way.

If I had been asked what might be achieved in these ten years I am pretty sure that I would not have said that there would be two key books on women's leadership published by members of the AWESOME committee and yet that is just what has happened. Rosie Ward, who became our membership secretary when Lucy Holt stepped down to become an incumbent, was then a Leadership Development Advisor on the staff of the Church Pastoral Aid Society (CPAS) with particular responsibility for developing women leaders. In 2008 BRF published her important book: Growing Women Leaders: nurturing women's leadership in the Church. It looked at all aspects of women's leadership from whether they should lead at all to the how it looks when they do and the examples of when they have from the New Testament right through Church history. After this, in 2010, IVP published a book by Clare Hendry and me (The Gender Agenda: Discovering God's plan for Church leadership) which rehearsed both sides of the biblical argument around whether women should lead and teach. It was written deliberately in a format which modelled a way of working together and listening to each other which we felt we found in AWESOME but which was rarely seen within the church. A way of listening which really gave time to the other and engaged respectfully and openly.

It was within this spirit of listening and working across boundaries that we were able to meet with Reform (the conservative evangelical group within the Church of England which is best known for its opposition to Women in the Episcopate) to begin to explore our differences. There is no doubt that this was precipitated by a desire to find a way through the issues around the 'women bishops' debate but it became very significant sharing and exploring with one another. It began with a meeting when we were able to acknowledge that there was a problem which needed to be addressed, a problem which was perceived differently on each side but which undoubtedly caused pain on both sides. Out of that honesty came the agreement that we should meet to discuss scripture and begin to thrash through the issues together. For us this was hugely significant. It felt that Reform being willing to commit to spend a day with us working at scripture meant that on some level a rubicon had been crossed. We had been accepted as evangelicals even if not as 'classic evangelicals', because they were acknowledging that we took scripture seriously enough to be worth engaging with.

In the end we met for three study days with three members of each grouping and three invited theological consultants equipping each group and helping to guide the discussion over a period of two years. Areas for discussion were agreed and papers were written and circulated before the meeting. The discussions were facilitated by the Bishop of Birkenhead, the Rt Revd Keith Sinclair. We covered all the predictable passages as well as issues surrounding hermeneutics and exegetics. For those interested the papers, accounts of the meeting and the statements can all be found on the AWESOME website (www.awesome.org.uk) under Resources and on the Reform website (www.reform.org.uk) under News for February 2012. The Final Statement is well worth reading as it highlights the differences which there clearly still were between us, in terms of theology, ecclesiology and hermeneutics but it also demonstrates just how far we came. I want to quote just one part of the Statement, not to privilege it above the rest but to demonstrate the significance of what was achieved:

> We have become aware how limited dialogue in this area has been among evangelicals for many years and some of the problems of misunderstanding and distrust that have arisen as a result. Despite our sometimes strong disagreements, our conversations in the context of the study of Scripture and prayer have been marked by growing friendship, respect and

understanding. We pray these qualities will develop and deepen more widely among evangelicals and within the Church of England as it considers legislation relating to women bishops.

These talks have been really vital on so many levels; there is little doubt in my mind that they, along with the books which have been published and talks given have helped to change the landscape. Important relationships have been forged which have meant that we have not been shouting across a great divide but are now actually having a conversation.

Of course Reform are not the only group within evangelicalism and there have been serious questions about how we relate to and encourage growth within other parts of the evangelical constituency. One of the really significant issues which we faced was that of appointments to evangelical livings, particularly by the evangelical patronage boards. It is fascinating that still today only 18% of stipendiary incumbents are women and, when we look at 'larger' churches, that is churches with a usual Sunday attendance of over 350 (adults and children) the picture is worrying. In 2005 all 172 'larger' churches were led by men; by 2008 two were led by women and between 2008 and 2010 another two had been appointed. This compares to the numbers of female Deans and archdeacons being appointed—5 Deans out of 47 and 23 archdeacons out of 128. This is significant because of the break-down of the 'larger' churches: the majority are evangelical, 9% self-designate as Reform, 35% Charismatic Evangelical, 32% 'Open' Evangelical; the rest are made up as follows: 7% Broad church; 4% Anglo-Catholic, 13% everything else (statistics from Brierley Consulting). This is important because for evangelicals their large churches are their flagships, their equivalent, almost, of cathedrals. It is in these churches that young people are particularly nurtured as they tend to be situated in university towns, working with students or in concentrations of young professionals. There is therefore an important question here about role models and inspiring young women to feel that it is ok for them to follow this sort of vocation. If all they see are men in these roles then they find it hard to imagine a woman doing it and making it work.

As a way of addressing this we held a consultation in collaboration with CPAS in which addressed this very question. We asked all the key patronage boards and invited them to think about the statistics and what women's experience of the application and interview process was. (All the papers from this consultation are available on the AWESOME website) We also asked them to consider a gender-blind application process, similar to that used in other professions. The fruit of this day is yet to be seen but there is no doubt that it gave many pause for thought and had led to some changes in practise. One of the key issues which we need to work at as a result is the encouragement of women to apply for these posts. Unfortunately, so many women feel that they have had such bad experiences in applying that others are put off. It is vital that this is broken and that women with the right experience continue to apply and so get into these posts – as well as others. Clearly there are also broader issues around appointments, but the patronage of the larger churches gives a snapshot of the bigger picture.

It has been exciting to see more ordained evangelical women doing theological research, entering what has been in so many ways a man's world. It has also been great as the numbers speaking at large events has slowly increased. There is, however, still a serious dearth on the Main Stage—for some reason it is still the case that lay women or female church leaders from overseas are trusted more than ordained women from our own context.

Alongside all of this we have been privileged to see our involvement within the national church grow. In 2011 Archbishop Rowan asked us to send 2 representatives to join a group he was establishing to advise him on women's ministry in the broadest sense. This is what later became known as the Transformations Group. Rosie Ward as vice-chair and I joined representatives from NADAWM (National Association of Deans of Women's Ministry), DARC (Deans, Archdeacons and Residentiary Canons group) and WATCH (Women And The Church); the group was later joined by Daphne Green, Chaplain and researcher to the Archbishop of York. It was vital that there was—and remains—an evangelical presence there.

One of the first things we did was to organise a conference, called 'Transformations' to look at and reflect upon all aspects of women's ministry. This took place in November 2011 and resulted in a key discussion document which went to the House of Bishops. There were a whole range of areas which needed further work ranging from terms of service (of, for example the discrepancy of maternity cover provision from diocese to diocese) to the discrepancy in the level of young vocations between men and women. As a group we were invited to give a presentation to the College of Bishops in September 2012 and out of that it was agreed not only to continue the Transformations work through addressing the key concerns but also to set up a Transformations Research Group working with Ministry Division to find more concrete statistics about the areas we were looking at, something which was necessary if we were to move forward.

Various members of the AWESOME committee have been involved in progressing the Transformations work. Both Rosie and I have been involved in setting up and working with the Research wing, which has been very exciting. Tamsin Merchant and I, along with of other remarkable AWESOME members worked with Liz Boughton and Catherine Williams at Ministry Division to organise a Vocations Day for Young Women and the Church. This was aimed specifically at the evangelical constituency, aware that in the under 30's age bracket the ratio of women to men coming forward is 2:7, and this inevitably has long-term implications within the church. It was an exciting day as we saw 65 young women from all over the country come together and get really enthused by the sight and experience of all those able women who genuinely love what they do and really believe that it is not only a great calling but it is also what God called them to.

There is no doubt that at NEAC4 God challenged me and changed my life. I would never have guessed that I would be involved in a group which networked and encouraged, resourced and spoke for ordained women. Nothing could have been further from my mind. And yet this has been one of the most thrilling gifts He has given me. It has been such a privilege to be called to serve this group, to watch it grow and develop – to see what God can do in such a short time with such a disparate group of people, with little or no resources. To work with the most amazing group of dedicated gifted women who are all-out for Christ. There have been some really tough times, like when the CEEC (Church of England Evangelical Council) having voted us on as a representative group, at the next elections decided that they did not need a group representing evangelical women and in our place voted on another conservative group. But I am challenged by the willingness of the women I work with to keep on keeping on. I am regularly humbled by the passion and the dedication of these women and by what God is doing through them. I am regularly challenged by their commitment to the gospel and to scripture and by their imagination and willingness to go not only the extra mile but way beyond that. The committees have been made up of gifted, busy women who are in challenging jobs on every level but who give sacrificially of their time—and money. I have never enjoyed any committee as much as I enjoy the fellowship of my AWESOME committees, we know each other well and laugh a lot—our friendships go very deep as does the prayer. We still don't have enough funding to make it possible for the committee to claim expenses, so everything we do we do through the sheer generosity and faith of those who believe that this is an important work of God. I am praying that this will change and that with the launch of Friends of AWESOME more funding will come in and we will be able to honour those who give so much in this vital work. I have learnt more than I can say from all of them and have seen God at work through them in countless ways.

I hope that this book will give you a snapshot of AWESOME—of what it means to have evangelical women ordained and faithfully serving within the church, faithfully sharing the gospel and ushering in the kingdom. There were so many other voices we could have heard and to choose any seemed invidious but it we wanted to give just an overview of the different ways in which our Awesome God is at work through the women He calls and empowers. I hope that what you read here will excite you as much as it excites me and that it will inspire you to go and discover more stories, to see what else our Awesome God is doing and to support and pray for those ordained evangelical women who are living all-out for Him and who know that "...we have this treasure in jars of clay, to show that this all surpassing power is from God and not from us".

God's Voice—calling
Jane Plackett & Suse McBay

Jane and Suse are both ordinands at St John's College, Nottingham, and both in their late twenties. Despite that, they have very different vocations! In the following chapter they discuss their call to ordination, their thoughts on identity and ministry, experiences of theological college and their hopes for the future.

Our journeys to faith

Jane

As you begin to explore ordination, you find yourself explaining over and over again the route that got you to this point. You say it to your diocese, your vicar, your bishop, your bishop's PA in the waiting room, your selection conference (three times in interview, fifteen times to each of the other candidates), your course mates (all of them at some point, most of them twice because they'll forget what you've told them, and it's the standard "getting to know each other" question). So by the 50th or so repetition you've begun to tire of your own story and after a while the significance of the things that you scrawled on your BAP form[1] which seemed so momentous and life-changing, and the acts of God that led you to this point have become just another dull part of your narrative.

After a while though, when you've been at college for a term, and you'll be asked something very specific, and you'll make a connection to your story and suddenly the whole experience comes alive again, and you're reminded of why you've endured everything in your life thus far, and now it all has a new perspective.

This happened for me during a meeting with the local council, sharing a vision for a project for which I hoped they might be prepared to consider getting involved in. He asked me simply "why", and this story came pouring out in a new way.

I'm aware my life is a privileged one. I didn't grow up in a wealthy home (despite my 'posh' accent

---

[1] BAP forms are the 'Bishops Advisory Panel' Form. This is a detailed account of your life, your education, your Christian faith, and your hopes for the future. The Panel are the selection committee that meet you at a residential selection conference at the end of your selection process, but you'll initially fill this in when you first meet with your Diocesan Director of Ordinands (DDO). An ordinand is the thing you are between being selected, and actually getting ordained!

and the love of country pursuits), but I grew up to a loving family and two parents that sacrificed so much of the things they loved in order for my sister and me to flourish. We lived in rural Cornwall, and walks, the beach, days climbing trees, and hours lost in the fields behind our family home have made me the person I am today. The fields are still where I've had some of my most powerful encounters with God, and the beach is still where I go to remind myself of my own insignificance.

Although not the typical "Christian home" my Mum attended church, and took me, and my sister along (and my amazing father occasionally put in an appearance too) until my sister was seven. From then, our attendance at church as a family diminished, and by my teens I was the only person who went.

At thirteen, I had privately decided that although the Christian life provided a solid moral framework, and some nice guidelines for living, there probably wasn't a whole lot more to it than that. I didn't stop going to church, after all, I liked the social aspect of it all, but I didn't see how I could make it the central thing in my life.

A couple of years later on a winter weekday night, I found myself at service for the Renewal of Baptismal Vows. I have no idea why I had decided to go—probably because I had something planned afterwards. As I said the words of the baptism service, I found myself crying—I couldn't have articulated why, and it would be more than a year until I would have the language to describe what happened – but I knew something had fundamentally changed.

Just over a year later, I went to a Christian festival in Somerset called Soul Survivor[2]. As I sat in the meetings and joined with this really young guy singing songs in a way that I didn't know was possible, as I watched people cry, and scream, and get down on their knees, and the Holy Spirit was explained to me, it suddenly gave me the language to describe the things of God I had seen previously.

I spent time asking God what He wanted from me. I love music – it's one my life's greatest passions – everything from Mozart to Miles Davis, and Prokofiev to Pink Floyd, I find it's the way to express the things on my heart and I'm thankful that it's so key not only now, but in the rich heritage of the church. I hoped God was calling me to be a worship leader, but didn't hear clearly so went off to London to study Civil Engineering, a degree I never actually completed. I

---

[2] Soul Survivor is a Christian youth event at the Royal Bath and West Showground. It has about 30,000 young people over four events at two sites. It's brilliant!

joined the Christian Union, and here was my first moment of discovery that other Christian students held (and vehemently so) radically different views to my own, and yet somehow, within the scope of Christendom, there's room for us all to thrive. There were moments of agony on CU committee meetings where we talked more about doctrine and creating the perfect mission statement than about worship, and looking back I realise that here's where God was revealing to me my heart for pastoring people, instead of rewriting mission statements and arguing about theological nuances. That's not to say that theological nuances aren't important – they really are. I'm thankful that hundreds of people have devoted years to scholarly Biblical research, and I'm thankful that they've written great books to summarise their discoveries. Unlike Suse, I'm delighted that the person doing that doesn't have to be me!

Suse

Unlike Jane, I don't really have any recollection of becoming a Christian. I don't remember a specific time when I wasn't a Christian or didn't have some degree of faith. There are certainly moments when I've learned something in my faith that made me wonder how I'd got so far without knowing it, but as far back as I can recall I've had some sense of the existence of God as revealed in Jesus. Like a lot of people, I grew up in a Christian family, in Oxford, and we went to church together every Sunday. It was the church where my parents got married, and my brothers and I were baptised and confirmed. I remember being present with a Bible, aged 5, and feeling very proud and grown-up. One of my other early memories was when I, aged 6, tried to convince my two friends that they could become Christians: all they had to do was be baptised by getting in the bath. It was that straight forward! Sadly, they weren't convinced. There were several significant moments for me in my youth when my faith took on a significant new dimension. Aged 11 or so, I prayed for a Youth Bible because I thought it would help me grow, but they were a bit expensive and it wasn't my birthday or Christmas. Not long later, I was off school because I was ill and went with my mum to her work. My mum left me with a Christian student she knew (I think her name was Laura) and after a bit of a chat, Laura told me that she had just bought a new Bible. Her old copy was a Youth Bible and she generously gave it to me. I loved it, and all the notes she had written in the margin encouraged me to engage with it personally and reflectively in a way she'll probably never know. It was very exciting seeing God answer my young prayer, especially given the stories of other Christians I'd read who'd seen God do extraordinary things and answer prayers in surprising ways. It was around this time that I got confirmed as well, which was a key marker for me in owning my faith for myself.

Throughout my teenage years my faith grew. It was a bumpy road, but I was blessed to be part of a church with a great youth-worker who took the time to mentor and encourage me. He helped me to learn to pray more deeply and encouraged me to serve at our church, St Clement's. There were lots of people around my age too, which helped. We put on monthly youth services, I played the piano in the worship band, and I led a few times too. The church wasn't perfect, like all churches, and sometimes far from it, but it was a place I could ask questions, learn a bit about the gifts God had given me and a place where I could belong. There were very few Christians at my school, and certainly none who I knew well, so church was really important for my faith. The other place where I found I belonged was on summer camp, specifically the Summer Theatre School that Riding Lights Theatre Company run in Yorkshire. I went numerous times (I forget whether I made double figures), and I loved doing drama with people who loved God too. I got my first opportunity to preach while I was there and I loved it: I knew I'd found something important that God had called me to do. I could finally relate to my friends there who knew they were going to go into acting. I'd always really enjoyed theatre but I knew they felt more passionate about it than I did. In preaching for the first time I experienced what I later realised was the same sense of vocation. This was it.

Learning and growing never stop. But I think the final piece of my growing up spiritually to the point of owning a distinctly adult faith was my gap year with Youth With A Mission in Australia and south-east Asia. I changed a huge amount in five months. The teaching was really good: I was challenged on all sorts of issues and encouraged to pray, read my Bible and listen to God. I began to engage more deeply with habits of repentance and forgiveness and the cost of discipleship. That said, looking back at old journals I'm not sure how much I really knew the implications of some of the prayers I was praying! It's been said before, but prayer should definitely come with a health warning.

Call to ordination: the highs and lows

Suse

I really did not, ever, want to be ordained. I know lots of people say that, but there was a time I wasn't sure any woman should be ordained, let alone me! Although full of passion for ministry and discipleship, I could not see myself as a vicar. It was the furthest thing from my mind. A good friend of mine from university can testify to it. I studied theology as an undergraduate, so people would frequently comment, 'Oh, so do you want to be a vicar then?' to which I would vehemently reply how out of order it was to assume just because I studied theology that I had to want to be a vicar. Outrageous! Or so I thought... I did know I felt called to teach in some capacity, but I also knew that teaching can take many forms, so I really didn't know what to expect. Anyway, I first took the idea of ordination seriously half-way through my third year of my degree. I prayed. I asked God for one of those moments where someone sits you down and says, 'Considering your gifts and talents I really think you should consider ___.' Within the week, Sally, an ordinand who studied theology at the same time as me, said these words to me. Only she filled in the blank with the dreaded word. Ordination. I argued with her profusely and gave five obvious reasons why I shouldn't, or couldn't, do it (I don't remember what they were). By this point I had thought through the Scriptures enough to be convinced that women should be ordained in some capacity, so I'd lost that as a defence. Sally patiently responded to my other objections. Even so, I wasn't convinced. But having had my prayer answered, I began to realise it was an itch I'd have to scratch sooner or later. Especially when everyone who I relayed the conversation to seemed to agree with my friend over me. I couldn't work out quite why the prospect of me being ordained was obvious to everyone else, and yet such a surprise to myself.

Shortly after finishing university I moved to St George's Church in Leeds to work as one of three interns, helping out with all sorts of things, though my main involvement was with the youth and student ministry. I'd been advised to wait till I was a few months out of university before I approached the diocese about ordination, which I did. But I still wasn't sure. I couldn't let the idea of ordination go, but neither did I particularly want to pursue it. On the other hand, the impatient part of me just wanted to get on with it and wanted the process to be as quick as applying for any normal job. As any ordained person will tell you, however, these things usually take a while. Looking back, I can see how far from ready I was, but at the time it seemed all too slow. I saw a vocations adviser for the diocese on two occasions and then she referred me to the DDO, Peter. I was then given a form. This form threw me entirely and I ignored it for the summer and told Peter not to expect to hear from me again. The questions were asking too much and I wasn't sure I was really 'called' enough to answer them. Thankfully another Peter (my chaplain from university) gave some wise advice and basically told me to get over myself and fill the thing in. So I did. I decided to push the door until it closed.

By this time I'd finished my internship, I had settled into life in Leeds, and then embarked on a PGCE in secondary RE. I knew school teaching was never going to be a whole life venture like it is for so many, but I learned more than I could ever express through the experience. It was as I started the PGCE that I was assigned an associate DDO. We met several times, each a couple of months apart. It wasn't always easy: sometimes I found it hard to communicate what I thought and felt, I think in part because it's never straight-forward to express these things, but also because I'd learnt the language of evangelical churchmanship and my associate DDO was far more Anglo-Catholic. Nevertheless eventually he said he thought I was ready for a local interview panel. As the panel approached, my first DDO moved away from the diocese and I was assigned another associate DDO, and a few months later I went to my local interview (around autumn 2009). This consisted of three interviews and a presentation. Amusingly the guy who was also being interviewed and I went against gender stereotypes for our presentations. I did mine on football and mission. He did his on spirituality and shoes! It was a surreal evening doing three separate interviews and being asked all sorts of different questions, about me, my family, my church experience and theological background. I found out early the next day that they decided to recommend me for the Bishop's Advisory Panel. I met with the chief DDO again two or three times, filled in even more paperwork, and then went to BAP.

BAP is like X-Factor boot camp, but without the competitive element (which is a relief because I can be very competitive). It was rather strange being in a retreat-like setting for three days, while at the same time knowing you're also being interviewed and observed. This was the final push of the door—o if it was what God wanted then this was it! The knowledge that it was in God's hands freed me to relax and simply be myself. I had felt a call to ordination and this was the place to test that calling and see if others could recognise it too. I'm not saying the Church of England's selection process necessarily gets it right all the time[3], but I was struck by the prayerfulness of those involved in my panel and I trusted God that would open the door if He wanted it opened. I found out afterwards I'd got through and subsequently received a three page report about myself as a result of the interview. Some parts were easier to hear than others; some was a little baffling, some food for thought, some affirming. The scariest thing for me was that the door had actually opened! That wasn't part of the deal—I was going to push the door until it closed. Didn't God realise that? It took me a few days to adjust to the news. The door had opened, which meant I had to go through it. I don't know if I thought it then, but looking back it reminds me of Gideon in Judges 6 with the doubt that went through my mind—how on earth could I ever be ordained! My flaws and doubts suddenly came into sharp focus, laid out before me: had God forgotten this stuff? Thankfully the initial panic subsided. I'm still aware of my flaws and doubts, probably more so than previously, but I've also been slowly learning that what matters most is that God is with me and He will equip me as necessary for the path ahead.

I did have some particular stumbling blocks that faced me as I went through this whole process. I was

---

[3] It's not for me to judge either way!

really quite confused by the long-argued headship debate. In part, because both sides sounded convincing: the biblical testimony is mixed and at first glance seems to conflict with itself. Also, the view that said that women could be the head of a congregation would obviously work to my advantage, and I didn't want people thinking I'd chosen it out of convenience so I tried really hard not to believe it. I didn't ever want to be accused of taking the easy way out. Plus there's the assumption by some that you do not take Scripture seriously enough if you are in favour of the ministry of women at every level in the Church. However, I read and re-read various points of view and came to the conclusion that if I was to submit to God and the testimony of the Bible then this is what it involved believing. There are many books on the subject, but the key text for me was Philip Barton Payne's book 'Man and Woman: One in Christ'. For me, the fact that he engaged with the Greek text and fully referenced his sources was incredibly helpful. I didn't agree with everything he said, but it was the final nail in the coffin of my previously held views.

The other stumbling block was my own imagination. I had grown up in a church where I saw two distinct categories: the vicar and the congregation. I didn't know my vicar particularly well, it was from a distance the gap seemed obvious, and I couldn't imagine myself doing what he did in the way that he did it. Furthermore, all the positive examples of vicars I had seen had been male, and whatever I did I knew I could never be a man! As a teenager I had seen female ministers, but none to whom I could relate. They seemed to be very different from me in personality type, and have a very different set of gifts. I learned that ordained ministry looked a certain way, and that way wasn't me. Thankfully this began to be unpicked through my undergraduate degree, where I met all sorts of women who challenged my preconceived notions, including a female chaplain who modelled something I could aspire to. Later, when working it through further in Leeds I found a paradigm that made much more sense to me than the shepherd and his flock: that of the captain of a football team. I'd been a captain of a football team. I knew what that meant. You are in the team, like any other, and yet you help make decisions and oversee the team's performance. You work closely with the manager to relay and work out the formation and plan of action he wants for the team. You are involved in the delivery of said plan. You set the example, you encourage, you step in when things get a bit hairy and the ref gets involved... I won't push the metaphor too far. But it made sense.

Jane

I first fleetingly considered ordination after I had witnessed a clergy member make a complete mess of a relationship with a youth group. I watched them bow to pressure from a congregation rather than doing the right thing, and arrogantly thought in the back of my mind "*I'm pretty sure I would make a better job of this...*" I didn't give it any more thought for about three years.

My Christian teaching until my early twenties had resulted in me concluding that women shouldn't really be ordained, and that probably, ideally, women should stay at home and raise a family. Biblically, and physically, it was all pretty obvious in my young mind! Three years of university studying Civil Engineering with a cohort of predominantly men taught me that I could thrive in a man's world, but to be taken seriously I would have to be not only equal to, but also better than, my male counterparts – particularly if I was going to insist on wearing skirts and heels to lectures. It's an interesting world.

After university I moved back to Cornwall for about a year before returning to the confines of the M25 to work for the youth organisation that had transformed my faith all those years previously. The years working for Soul Survivor were brilliant. It was, and still is, a place where young leaders are equipped to fulfil their potential. I'm still so thankful that for a few years my day job was getting to minister to teenagers, and facilitate their growth and development. I also got to do this with a team of people that were an example of love and of Jesus to me, and who loved me, fostered my gifts, and gently rubbed away at my more abrasive sides, and spiky edges. Forgive the sentimentality at this point, but I owe the team of people around me for those years a great deal of gratitude for shaping so much of the person I am today.

Over my time there I began to see how vast ministry life could be for both men and women, and I slowly became more and more confident about what I, as a woman, had to offer. I also found space to just be me, to learn to be a girl again, and to not constantly be pushing to be stronger, more creative, more disciplined, more authoritative, or more intelligent than my male colleagues. God then started to speak to me about my future. For about two years, I kept reading Ezekiel 37, coming across it when people sent me cards, at church, and odd services I ended up at, at conferences, people praying prophetically and reading it to me – it was a verse there all the time.

One summer, driving down to prepare for the summer events at Soul Survivor, after spending two weeks in South Africa desperately trying to figure out what God was asking me to do with my life, I gently mused to two close friends and colleagues that thoughts of ordination had been on my mind! We laughed about it and I put the thought aside. A few weeks later I was sitting under a tree with a Hugo Anson, an amazing man who runs the Grassroots Trust and is one of the most prophetically gifted people I know—to the extent it slightly scares me to spend time with him because I'm so aware that God may speak to me through him, and that I may not want to hear it.

Sitting under a tree, he asked "What's your 'life verse'?" It wasn't an expression I'd ever heard. I'd been reading the book of James at the time, and God was challenging me on how I used words. I shared it. He looked at me and said "that's not your life verse – I'll come back to you after everyone else". I felt a bit baffled, and slightly embarrassed. Then Ezekiel 37 – the Valley of the Dry bones – was the story that came to mind. I shared this. He immediately said "Jane, have you ever thought about becoming a vicar?" My friends laughed, I felt shell-shocked, promptly decided that it couldn't be God, and tried to shelve the thought.

Over the coming months this verse kept cropping up everywhere. Each time I read it, God showed me the same picture, and each time I became aware on some level that I was detaining the inevitable.

Two years on, I came back from the summer events and came down with a virus, and a resulting post virus illness wiped me out for nearly two months. I followed the same pattern: Going to work, coming home, and going to bed before ten – unheard of for me! Two months passed, and my friends were praying for me on the sofa one evening. I felt God say to me "You'll get better when you do what you're told" – I felt so much like I think Jonah may have done in that moment – knowing that God had been asking me to do something all this time, and knowing I had chosen to ignore it because it wasn't really the thing that I had in mind. I phoned our newly ordained youth pastor to pop round for tea – I think I'd unnerved him by wanting to see him urgently. By the following day I was better, and I believe God healed me physically, as He healed my heart.

The next bit of the process for me (chatting to the vicar, and seeing the vocations advisor) went really fast. I had the benefit of a hugely broad background of churches which was helpful particularly when you're in a less than orthodox Anglican church, such as Soul

Survivor. It means you have a good understanding of what it means to be an Anglican, rather than just your own expression of Anglicanism. After one meeting with a vocations advisor I was put in touch with a DDO[4], and I'm ashamed to admit here that I ignored his calls for six months. Being a vicar was so far from what I'd intended to do, the realities of getting to this stage this quickly was too much for me to cope with.

The process of selection was gruelling and invasive. There is no topic beyond the scope of your DDO's questioning: from your sexuality to your finances; your relationships; your health; your emotional robustness; your intellect; your character and your personality are all scrutinised. You give away huge amounts about yourself to this person, and are likely to share things with them that up until this point you may not have shared with anyone else. You bare your heart, and it can be a vulnerable experience.

It's also an immensely rewarding one when this relationship works well (I had one excellent DDO, and the other with whom I found the relationship incredibly challenging). You'll read together, learn together, pray together, explore together. I shed a lot

---

[4] Your DDO is the Diocesan Director of Ordinands, your 'go-to' person for all your questions and your coach and mentor prior to your interview.

of tears too. Being a bit of a weeper by nature, all extreme emotional situations make me cry – whether I'm furious, or broken-hearted, scared, excited or joyful – I cry. Putting so much of yourself on the line can be an emotional experience.

Then there's the selection conference. Some people hate them, but I LOVED mine! Lots of new people, nice food, nice town, good coffee shops close by (if you're in Ely, at least), and a lot of time talking about myself – bliss! By this stage you've shared your most hidden heart on more than one occasion so it's beginning to get easier to share your hope for the church and for your future. This is the culmination of months of hard work, so I decided to enjoy it.

The last words of advice from my DDO were "Jane, be yourself, but for heaven's sake, please don't be too much yourself!" I totally ignored her advice. I didn't really want to do this, and if the Anglican Church wanted me, then they needed to know it was 'me' that they were getting. I was the fullest version of myself, warts and all, at my conference. When asked what I'd do if I didn't get in, they had to ask me to stop with my list of possibilities! This was never the journey I would have chosen for myself, but having got just this far – one year into three years of training at college, plus the curacy afterwards—I wouldn't change it.

Over all of this time, God kept drawing me back to Ezekiel 37, and over time the way I saw it changed. If I rewrote this passage as God has revealed it to me up to now, it would be a little bit like this:

> *"Then the Spirit came on me, and took me into the poorest parts of the Nation and I saw desperate families, children from broken homes not achieving their potential in school, disadvantaged by their family situations. I saw the lonely, the addicts, the self harmers and the suicidal – people broken, and dry of any hope. God said to me 'Jane, can these people have a different kind of life?' I said, 'Lord, I don't know, they seem so desperate.'*
> *Then God said, 'Sort this out'. And I said, 'But how do I start?' God replied, 'Provide for them, organise parenting classes, homework clubs, financial advice clinics, life skills classes. Go into schools and teach young people about their value, build community, build family, fill your home with people, network Christian counsellors, be a friend and an ear, get taken advantage of and delight in it, for neither your time nor your money really*

belong to you.' I heard a rattling sound as I saw peoples' lives slowly come back together.

Then he said to me 'Jane, tell these people what really changes their lives, tell them to ask me to breathe life into their hearts.' So I did. I saw people whose practical needs had been met in the church go from death into life as they came to know Jesus. I saw people leave their old ways behind, I saw people full of the Holy Spirit, and both they and I knew that only God could have done it.

And God said to me, 'My dwelling place will be with them forever. I will be their God, and they will be my people.'

I can't say it any better than that. It's the dream that gets me out of bed in the morning. I long to see the church back at the centre of community, and I just hope that's not naive.

Identity and Ministry: what we are passionate about

Jane

I'm still learning what I'm passionate about. I know that sounds silly, but I find as I learn more not only about God through the Bible, but also as I learn about politics, social justice, trafficking, poverty, education, science, and even baking that I'm still changing. Sometimes I feel completely overwhelmed as there are so many areas of ministry where I can imagine myself working forever. I once felt that I'd been called to rural ministry[5]. I'm rediscovering that I have a passion for young men and women that I didn't realise was so profound until getting back involved with youth work again at college. I cry over suicide rates in young men. I cry as I read about adoption and foster rates for boys particularly over the age of eleven. I cry when I read about young women who think that a pregnancy is the thing that will give them purpose and value. My heart physically hurts when girls tell me they watch porn so they can understand what their boyfriends expect of them. I get really frustrated when I see natural leaders un-mentored,

---

[5] I'm reading this back—by 'once', I'm actually referring to just six months ago—things change, and you change, so quickly at theological college as God shows you more of who He is, that weeks can feel like hours. Conversely, one awful lecture can feel like it takes a week...

and their leadership viewed as awkwardness or bossiness. I get so disheartened when I see young men and women with all the benefits of wealth, influence and education not realise that they have the potential to change the world, and all they have to do is give their time and energy to God and say to him "have Your way with me", and then listen and obey when He gives them an answer.

Ezekiel 37 is still the Bible passage that I go back to when I'm asking God to reveal more of His heart to me, or when I'm confused, frustrated, angered by the way the Church of England does things. I long to see God use His church to change the nation, if not the world, and so, when I'm wondering why there just seems to be so many things I could spend myself on, and not enough hours in the day I remember that it's because I've sung and prayed, probably a hundred times, "break my heart for what breaks yours". When I ask God that, He's going to do it—which leaves me broken for so many different things, in the same way that His heart is, and I can only ever understand in part the things that burden God for His people.

Suse

When I read through Jane's description of her sense of identity and purpose within ministry it reminds me just how grateful I am for the diversity of the body of Christ! The direction God is calling me is thankfully not the same direction He is calling most people—if the church was full of ministers like me it'd be a lot poorer for it. I am really encouraged when I hear of someone called to do something totally different from me, something I know is absolutely not what God is calling me to do. Why? Because sometimes I feel I ought to have a certain gift, or ought to serve in a certain way, because the needs are so great. One of the hardest things I've had to do was leave secondary teaching. There was so much opportunity to offer Jesus' love to children whose lives have been hurt by all manner of things. Yet at the same time I knew it wasn't where God was calling me, I knew I couldn't sustain that lifestyle very long, and I knew my obedience mattered more to God than what seems fruitful and makes for a better testimony. So when I come across someone who sees those sorts of needs and it's clear that they have the gifts, the love, the patience, and the experience to minister in such a way, it makes me rejoice.

As a child, I read biographies of ministers and missionaries and thought that's what it looked like to be obedient to God. I spent a gap year in Australia with a missions organisation and found it really hard to see the part that I play in the body of Christ, because it wasn't as exciting or as directly effective as I wanted it to be. It wasn't as cutting edge as my friends. When I was away camping in the outback, however, I had a series of surprise encounters that made it so clear even I had to take notice. God had called me, in some capacity, to teach. It started the morning after a guy prayed for me about the future and my theology degree. I woke up with an unspoken, innate sense that I was made to teach. Later that day, one of the leaders who I'd never talked to, came up to me during another time of prayer and shared, emphatically, that God was calling me to teach. I forget all the details, but during those weeks I became sure that was what God was saying, but still I had no idea of the context and had a sure sense that whatever it was, it would definitely be a surprise.

Since then, the call to teach has grown and taken a deep root in my heart. The best way I can explain why I am so passionate about teaching is because I profoundly believe that growing in knowledge of the truth of the gospel changes, transforms and liberates. Being a teacher starts with being a learner. For me, learning theology has never (or very rarely) been tedious and dull. I find it fascinating, stimulating and it leads me to worship. It leads me to repentance. I don't think everyone's wired to learn that way, but if I am, I *want to share it with others. One of the greatest revelations for me was realising that learning doesn't have to be about saying 'look, come and see how much I know' but rather 'I'm discovering these things, so come, look, and talk with me about it!'*

One of the major surprises for me has been that part of my call to ordination is also to research, and specifically the New Testament and second Temple Judaism. I would never have imagined that I would end up doing a PhD in biblical studies, and certainly not the New Testament. I would never have thought that I would be the person to study footnotes and discover the joy of a decent bibliography. It seemed to me that it could only be properly done by a certain sort of man. Discovering (through a whole other story) that God wanted me to do such a PhD was the most exciting, obvious and yet surprising realisation. I've always loved the Bible, loved Greek, loved commentaries and biblical dictionaries, etc. Yet I never thought that could be where God would want me. Not in the slightest. So when it became patently obvious that was where He wanted me, it made complete sense, yet was a total surprise. It was the best gift, but one I never thought I would be given. It's a privilege. It's certainly only a small segment in the breadth and depth of church life and activity, without the rest it is nothing, but in its proper place it's really quite beautiful.

Life at theological college: expectations and reality

Suse

My expectation of training at St John's College, and the idea of theological college in general, was a little different than usual as I'd spent my undergraduate degree at Wycliffe Hall, Oxford. That isn't to say my expectations were accurate, however! While there are certain things that remain pretty constant about living in community, both the joys and the irritations, there have been plenty of differences. As an undergraduate I was only studying academic theology and doing no formal ministerial training. Although I chose to get quite involved in worship and joined a fellowship group, it was not expected of me. My experience of St John's has been significantly different from Wycliffe and I cherish both as a place I've called home at different times in my life. Perhaps part of the reason for the level of difference is because I feel like a different person: I've learned so much in the intervening years. On the other hand, I do think it is probably a healthy caution to any theology graduate to be aware that ordination is a whole different kettle of fish from studying theology as an academic discipline. Neither one is better than the other: it just affects you in different ways. At least it has in my experience.

Theology as an academic discipline challenged me to think more deeply than I had ever done before. I had to learn to argue, interacting with other theologians and thinkers whose works I read. Most significantly the things I thought I knew from Sunday school and my naive reading of the Bible as a youth were upturned. The fundamentals remained the same, but it was quite unsettling to learn about the process of how different biblical books were written and how they were gathered together into the form we now read. The prospect of a single biblical book having more than one author was difficult for me: I like things to be clear cut and in nice, neat boxes. But that's not necessarily how the Bible is. You only need to learn a biblical language to see that. There are many decisions that have to be made in the process of translation which reveal just how unclear certain things can be. Just how did the conquest of Canaan take place? What light do ancient near eastern stories of creation shed on the purpose of Genesis 1-11? Who was Darius the Mede in the book of Daniel? When was Daniel written? How do I understand prophecy in the Old Testament? How do I make sense of the differences in the gospels, both in events in Jesus' life and teaching as well more generally the different emphasis that the gospel authors give? The questions go on and on. I found myself realising that I had placed my faith in my assumptions of how to read the Bible, in the categories I was reading it within, rather than really looking, stopping, and thinking about the implications of the content and the purpose for which it was written.

Life as an ordinand at St John's has been quite different. The word 'formation' is used frequently as part of the process of being at college; so much so it becomes a bit of a cliché. But there's a reason it's talked about so much. A bishop in my first year talked about theological college as being like a car being parked in a lay-by, having its engine re-done. I saw ordinands at Wycliffe going through the experience, and I've encountered it myself at St John's. I have felt undone, less able, less equipped and less confident at times here than I have ever felt before. I've experienced emotions I didn't know I had, and I've questioned God on levels I didn't know possible. I've been outright angry with God at times. The process of being undone by God is painful, as He strips us back layer by layer. Time and again I've realised how much I define myself by my reactions to things I've experienced, both the good and the bad. Letting go of who I want to be and my pride, and learning to live in Christ is a generous gift of grace, but one that comes at a cost and with tears. It's part of discipleship throughout the whole of life, of course, but theological college offers the time and space and the support to go a little deeper.

The final thing to say about my experience of theological college is how different it is to study as a research student. I will have been at St John's for 4 years by the time I finish here, which is twice as long as the average student. Doing a PhD both affects how I relate to the community and it affects me personally in terms of the character demanded by the task. It's an isolating experience: nobody quite understands your subject, and few grasp why you'd ever want to spend so much time on such a specific thesis and it places you in a funny kind of limbo. I am an ordinand and so share the same hopes and fears of ministry as any ordinand. Yet I am also learning to be an academic and contribute to knowledge in a particular field, so I feel at times more akin to the teaching faculty in college. There are positives and negatives to this: it's a peculiarity of the job. It is strange to be sat in a library all day, but it's really not an ivory tower. Sometimes sitting with only a book to distract me is the last place I'd want to be: it's hard to hide from yourself in a library. Life as a teacher gave me much more opportunity to hide from reality! I love my research, and I'm sure God has called me to it. How that relates exactly to my future I don't know, and I'm also sure I'm not ready for my future yet either. Thankfully all I need to do is be faithful with what God has given me today.

Jane

Like Suse, I love to learn. I love to read, I love to research, but if you left me in a room full of books all day it would be almost my worst nightmare. I'm an extrovert, I learn best through conversation, face to face teaching and through trial and error. Revelation about myself comes through others, not through facing myself when left alone. A day in isolation with a book is reserved for only times when I'm 'peopled out' or when I have an essay due—even then, if there's the option of studying in a cafe, or with others, then that would be my preferred environment. I do, however, need people like Suse to both challenge and resource me. She makes me ask difficult questions of myself and of scripture, and forces me to focus on the thinking not the doing.

Theological college is brilliant. I'm not saying that there aren't ghastly and difficult days – there are. And there are other times when you walk away unsure you can believe a word the Bible says, the bedrock of your faith is chipped away, and you wonder for a few hours whether or not everything you've ever thought about Jesus is wrong and the whole structure of your life is going to fall down, or at best, be permanently destabilised.

Thankfully so far for me these moments have been fleeting, and staff, tutors and chaplains have been there to scoop us up off the floor and set us straight again, and make a few patchy repairs to our theology to allow us to carry on without feeling totally bereft. There's a place for quickly coming to recognise that saying that faith has its mysterious elements isn't a cop out – it's an essential element of pursuing truth and asking difficult questions without losing faith.

So the studying is great, but community is hard. Much, MUCH harder than I expected. There are more rotas than you could have dreamed of, and having so many gifted leadership in one cohort regularly has its challenges. Thankfully, your time at college is comparatively short, and so you're unlikely to ever have to be among so many natural leaders again.

Taking yourself out of 'real life' and coming away for a significant period to pray, develop good life habits, to learn, to read and to make lifelong friends is such an incredible opportunity. Those first weeks of being out of leadership, and free from pastoral responsibility I found to be incredibly freeing – I LOVED not having to plan services, look after people, or sort out font or formatting problems, but most people really struggled with being in a new context and not getting to exercise the leadership, and taking the authority that they were used to. The first term was pretty gruesome – a lot of 'intentional' relationship building, lots of insecurity, lots of rediscovery of self – it's tough, and a big adjustment, but living in close proximity to others means there's no room to hide oneself or one's issues from colleagues – and once you've got used to it, you quickly become aware of how much of a blessing that is.

Studying theology, reading, writing and thinking is now your way of life, and it's a real privilege. To make it better, you get to do it with a group of people that you're in community with, committed to, and you genuinely believe are the hope of the Anglican Church – that's pretty incredible.

Looking to the future: challenges and hopes

Jane

The future. That's terrifying.

Those who know me well know that I'm a hideous over thinker, so I think about the future a whole lot. I allow all kinds of scenarios to play out in my mind, and I imagine the consequences of them all—my mind is always racing at a frantic pace.

I'm aware that I set unattainably high standards for myself and for others. I really struggle with mediocrity, but I'm learning to live constantly not reaching the high targets I set for myself and for others. I like to strive for the very best, except in essays – those you just need to pass. I like other people to be the best that they can be, but I'm often easier on others than on myself when they don't quite get there. So you can see that there are some paradoxes that I'm still working out here.

I'm 28, and I thought that I'd never particularly wanted a family, but somewhere along the line I must have imagined that I would be married by now, with at least a couple of kids. Wednesday nights at St John's are for the whole college family—husbands, wives, children and teenagers. Sometimes those nights for single students can be really tough, especially because at St John's Wednesday Chapel comes at the end of

'Spirituality Day' which is our weekly quiet(ish) day of reflection and formation. By 8pm, you can feel emotionally wrung out, and I know it's not uncommon for there to be tears before bedtime for more than one of us.

Life hasn't turned out how I imagined, and I fully expect that it will continue not carrying on in the way I expect for as long as I'm obedient to God! I might meet someone who makes my world a brighter, better place, and me a stronger, bolder, more courageous girl. Or, of course, there is the very real possibility that I might not. As a fairly strong minded, opinionated woman, (I'm regularly told that I would be "a lot to take on"—don't even get me started on that!) and with a disproportionate ratio of men to women in the church (and not in favour of the ladies) I'm realistic that simple mathematics suggests that God may call me to singleness. If I'm completely honest, this isn't the struggle for me that it is for some of my close friends, but it is still a disappointment that I have to give back to God every three months or so, trusting that He has it in hand. So much as I want to have a large home, full of rowdy boys (ideally—not that we get to choose!), three dogs, and an Aga, I would rather walk in God's way for me, knowing that it is the best possible path, than choose my own route and live knowing that life has never been all that it could have been[6]. I don't say that lightly but I want to acknowledge this struggle because even for me, when you're a single girl, and almost everyone on your course is married, most of the ladies in your year group will be those married to your colleagues and many are pregnant or with under 2's. As a result your own insecurities will crop up pretty regularly, and if it's an area where you're really struggling, it's definitely an area you'll need to prayerfully prepare yourself for prior to starting college.

So overall, my hopes for the future are quite small. I hope to be obedient. I hope to keep listening. I hope to be courageous enough to believe that God can do the impossible in partnership with me and the church. I hope to be tenacious enough to plod on when I'm in circumstances I never imagined I would be in. I hope that God will make me into the kind of person that young people will aspire to be. Primarily, I hope that on the day I die, I will know that I've lived a life as obedient, as loving, as merciful, and as full as it was possible for me to do, and that I love Jesus more

---

[6] I recognise that of course, that some people would want to have a theological discussion with me over the idea of free will and this statement as a whole. Put it aside. Go with the spirit of the statement.

then than I do now. If we get there, trite as it sounds, I'll be pretty made up.

Suse

When it comes to personal hopes for the future, I agree with Jane. I hope to be obedient in what God asks of me, however surprising or difficult or wonderful it might be. I hope more than anything that I live from a personal, knowledge of God's love in mind, heart, body and soul, and know the freedom therein to love well and live in abandon. There are always practicalities to contend with. By the time this is published I'll be getting used to being married and then soon after working out how to balance marriage and ministry and completion of a PhD. I never really factored in the idea of marriage so it's all a bit of a surprise really. Definitely a good surprise, though! Unlike Jane, I've never really wanted children. Whether that will change I don't know. If it does it will present a new set of issues, different from those of being married, and different from those of being single. But challenges are a fact of life, whatever the situation. There's always a balance to be struck. I hope I don't get unduly caught up in the detail of it all.

When it comes to church and my vocation, I am excited, daunted, and hopeful. Being part of the church and knowing the many faithful who go before me makes me aware of the responsibility we have to keep the faith and pass it on, and especially those within leadership. I want to learn from those who are more experienced than me, and the example they set of imitating Christ. I'm sure that being faithful into the future is about learning from the experiences of those from centuries past, from those a generation above me as well from my own personal history.

In terms of wider church issues, it's been roughly 20 years since women were first ordained as presbyters in the Church of England and, in the last few years, there has been a lot of work to try and figure out how to change things so women can be bishops too while maintaining space for those who have a different theological position. While things have stalled a bit in recent months, it'll inevitably happen, and so it should. Subsequently there'll be other challenges facing the Church of England, some of which we know and some that will undoubtedly surprise. But again, I hope that as God's people we bear the responsibility faithfully. My biggest hope for the church worldwide, and where I find myself in the Church of England, is that we love one another as Christ loved us, even across differences. That love may not be easy, and may involve hard words to hear as well as generous ones, but my prayer is that we will have the humility for the task.

Concluding thoughts

Jane

Coming to college gave me hope for the church. Over the first few weeks of getting to know everyone I found a group of people with incredible passion for the church – and not a green, naive passion, but one that for many was grown out of dealing with a disappointment, or a frustration of their experience of church thus far. It was realistic – not wanting to change the world overnight, but wanting to see the church bring hope.

I also found a whole range of skills and talents. I found people called to Cathedral ministry; those who have a burden to do traditional Anglican ceremonies beautifully, and those like Suse who have a passion for learning more, and want to spend themselves sharing that with others. I found artists and academics, sportsmen and scientists, all with unique callings to ministry, all different, and all who had found a space in the Anglican Church.

At college you find for the first time a group of people who shared your heart, and saw the Anglican Church as a way to bring transformation to our nation. Our approaches may be wildly different: for example, for me, I would think it will involve young people, and a practical, transformational, hands-on approach, rooted in community. For Suse, it's sharing her passion for scripture, for Biblical languages and, perhaps, her own spiritual journey, with those whom she teaches. All to equip them for the specific ministries to which they're called or, as one of our lecturers put it the other week, to "love students into the stature to which they're called".

This is a retreat time for God to do a transforming work in us, preparing many people with desperate visions for the callings they have ahead, and it's a privilege to be here.

Suse

Looking back over our respective stories it's a real inspiration to hear how God has been at work in Jane's life and how He has brought her to this point. While we both have a similar determination and passion in life and faith, the differences between us are quite marked. There are familiar strands in her story of God's hand at work. But less so with respect to the ministries to which we feel God is calling us. It'd be fun to do this again in 50 years and see how our lives unfold! Our differences teach me something as well. Jane and I offer different gifts and skills (I particularly like Jane's baking...). We are quite different people, and I hope that I both learn from Jane herself, but also from the different picture she offers me of what a minister looks like. It's really easy to think it has to look a certain way, and I'm not just talking about the traditional white, male model. I hope that people see our different stories and examples (as with the whole of this book) and use the space between them to re-imagine the type of people God calls to ordination: to see that ministers, like the whole of the church, should be an odd-looking bunch of peculiars who may have little in common except Christ.

Listening to others and voicing the Spirit

Sally Hitchiner

They say your Christian vocation is often hallmarked by how you found faith. I found faith, or at least personal faith, when I was a young person on a holiday camp. I was the type of child who went along with things. When I was at school I went along with being one of my friends, when I went to church I managed to blag my way through. One summer I was singing hymns in a children's meeting and suddenly I had the strongest sense that I didn't believe a word I was singing. It was such a powerful experience and I felt so uncomfortable about it that I sat down and stopped singing. And at that moment I decided to start a quest: to take a few months to work out if God and Jesus and all that was true. I read the Gospels over and over and I started going to church regularly. Mostly I wanted just to watch people, to see if they really meant what they were saying or if they were just putting on an act too. By the end of a few months I begrudgingly admitted that it was real, that there was a God, that Jesus was who he said he was and that I had to live the rest of my life in light of that. Excitement and hope filled my little school uniform and I regularly convinced my friends to stay in at lunch-break to do Bible-studies that I made up for them. It seemed like the world's best kept secret: God is kinder and more involved, following God is not about becoming a boring clone but celebrating diversity and endless interest, and that there is hope for every person, every situation that doesn't require you to pretend it's not that bad or to blag your way through. I later learnt that there are words for the hunches I had about God: the incarnation, the trinity and the resurrection. These concepts have influenced just about everything I've done for God since and they're the writ large as I look back over my ordained life. In fact they could be described as chaplaincy.

For me, chaplaincy has taken many forms. My approach to being a parish priest was so involved in my local community that when the riots struck Ealing I knew them well enough to play a part in coordinating the clear up response and representing the community in the following consultations. Chaplaincy affects how I work in the media: I'm told I have been on television, radio or in national newspapers more times over the past 2 years than almost any other priest in the UK. I spent a year as an Anglican chaplain in Oxford University and now work full time coordinating the large multi-faith chaplaincy at Brunel University London.

OXFORD

I was accepted to train for ordination at a relatively young age. The average age for ordinands in the UK at the time was 42. I was 25, not the youngest but on the younger end. History shows us that God values and calls people of all ages and for me it was just the right age. I loved my three years studying theology. Oxford pushed us through essays and topics just fast enough to grasp concepts but with no room to get bored. My time spent at Wycliffe was mostly a heady dream of tradition and expectation. We were walking the streets of world changers and who knew what we would go on to do.

After training but before ordination I was offered the opportunity to spend a year working half time as Assistant Chaplain at St Peter's College Oxford and half time as Associate Chaplain for the Oxford Pastorate. It seemed too good an opportunity to miss. I told people that in my first degree my mother would roll her eyes and tell me I was never going to get a job just having coffee with people and organising religious meetings... I proved her wrong! As well as running the chapel services and being available for pastoral support for students, I had rooms in halls, I ate with the students, I spent all but my day off socialising with students—it was quite an intense experience: a baptism by fire into the concept of incarnational ministry and I learnt a lot very quickly.

On one hand being an Oxford chaplain is breathtakingly simple. I had 400 students almost all of whom ate in the same dining hall 3 times a day. I was given a generous food budget and quickly developed a ministry of eating! I'd often arrive at the start of the 2 hour meal slot and sit and eat salad talking to whoever sat opposite me. I'd ask about how the rowing was going or the drama society or whatever else they were into and eventually they'd have a think of things that I might be interested in. Invariably the conversation moved towards religion. "I had a Christian friend at school" they'd start "Oh were they nice?" I'd follow. "Yes, they were nice actually."... Or they'd start with "I've been meaning to ask someone religious about something, how can you square earthquakes with a belief in an all powerful being?" I must have spent 5 or 6 hours a day just chatting,

chatting and eating. I quickly realized two things: that it was worth investing time reading up about apologetics and that I needed to join a gym!

Working for the Oxford Pastorate continued the feeling that I was standing on the shoulders of giants. C S Lewis had been the patron back in the 1950s and the then chaplain, Miss Stella Aldwinckle, had set up a Socratic Club based on Socrates' ideas that truth was to be found in discussion. It was inspirational to have had a bright capable woman doing my job all those years ago and I felt her presence snapping at my heels if I was ever afraid to throw myself in to academic discussion on atheism.

I discovered a fair few atheists among my students at my meal time conversations. Chatting over an early breakfast David, a second year Politics, Philosophy and Economics undergraduate confided that he'd been thinking about his convictions about the lack of God. "If I'm honest about my beliefs" he said bleakly "I should really commit suicide. I'm not about to do it, but that's just because I'm not a very good atheist". This conversation rang around my ears for days. I'd never heard a 19 year old sound so hopeless about life. Regardless how many generations of them have gone before them to mediocre suburban careers, Oxford undergraduates mostly believe that they will change the world, they will be the ones to bring about radical shifts in society. But this young man unlocked a deep honesty. The Christian students held their meetings, just getting around to answering questions students outside the church had been asking 30 years ago, the atheist society had their meetings misquoting the bible and hailing with strawmen of faith and the world rolled on with students like David at risk of becoming a "better atheist".

I decided to bring the two groups together. I gathered David and a few of the other atheists I'd got to know, and a few of the more open minded CU members, booked the upper room of a small coffee shop in the centre of town and restarted the Socratic Society. It was quite a success, within a term it had grown to 3 different groups meeting across the city and Dawkins was no longer welcome at the Secular society because of his intolerance towards religious groups. As far as I know David has yet to become a better atheist.

"I'm not trying to sound rude" started James the law post grad after a few weeks of getting to know me "but why do we need a chaplain in a secular institution like this?" His face was earnest, not cocky, so I tried to respond with an equally sincere answer.

"I think places like this need somewhere to go, someone to talk to who isn't assessing you. It needs someone pushing the idea that you are valuable no matter what grades you get, no matter how cool you are."

"Is that what Christianity is about?"

"Yes, yes it is" I said, realising that I'd stumbled in to a conversation about grace. "It's about God loving each of us irrespective of what we've done or not done and making it possible for us to be in relationship with God." I couldn't believe how corny I was sounding. I often ended up channelling 50s evangelists but somehow it made sense in those contexts. It didn't sound as cliché to fresh ears... at least I hope it didn't... they could have just been being nice!

The chapel services exploded. Somehow it got into the minds of the first years that when you went to Oxford you took up rowing and every Sunday evening you went to chapel before formal hall. At one point we had a regular congregation of over 150 students. It didn't last forever, gradually they got talking to other friends and realised that it wasn't that cool to go to chapel but we still had 40 or so who kept coming, touched by the music or wanting a chance to connect with God in ways they found hard to express.

Chaplaincy is often about the unseen. For me it requires greater dependence on God the Holy Spirit than parish church work. You have to just create spaces and trust that God is working. God invariably is working. I had countless stories of students like Adam who wondered into the back of evensong over heard the hymn "Abide with me" and wept as he told me afterwards that this is what he's longed to find, a God who would abide with him: the incarnate God.

SOCIAL MEDIA AND THE RIOTS

It might seem strange to include a section on social media in a chapter on chaplaincy but it's been as real an experience of chaplaincy as any. This was never more the case than when, half way through my curacy, the riots hit London (and much of the rest of the UK) in the summer of 2011. It was the holiday week of the summer and almost every vicar in Ealing was away. I was at home when I heard the first shouts outside my window. I looked to see a group of boys running down my street. Ealing is mostly on Twitter so I checked to see if anything was happening. It was quite a surprise to find warnings that we were the next place to be hit. I called the other members of the staff team to make sure we could cancel any meetings we had on that night. The last thing I wanted was little old ladies venturing out to church! I went out to have a look around and make sure the vulnerable in our parish were okay. Shop keepers were boarding up their windows as if a cyclone was about to hit. Down the road in Ealing Broadway I could see cars on fire. Buses stopped and kicked out all their passengers, unwilling to carry on their route. A guy from church who had come with me helped them work out how to walk home through the backstreets. It felt like a war zone and eventually it felt like there was nothing left to do but go home and wait.

By then Facebook messages had started to come in from members of my church. "What can we do to help?" "I'm sure I can take the day off work if needed", "My colleagues want to help too". Working with Ealing Council we coordinated part of the clean up. We ran a prayer meeting that morning as normal and arranged for the church to be open for distressed residents to come in to light a candle or have a cup of tea and someone to talk to. We put up a huge sign saying "CHURCH OPEN" and I heard more stories of people noticing that than any other signs we've ever put up! I had calls from the media and did a string of interviews in between going around the shop keepers with members of my church to ask how they were and offer comforting bible verses that someone in my church had prepared. I spoke to the other church leader left in Ealing and we decided to hold a prayer meeting where the riots had struck. This became huge. I think it must have been because it was the first one in the UK. With all the local vicars on holiday there was no one to have planning meetings with so we were able to move fast and got it organised within twenty four hours. Four hours in we had police/council clearance, six hours in someone from the Methodist church had heard about it and offered their outdoor PA system, someone from the local Pentecostal church called around the local press to tell them what was happening. We called around all the local Christian denominations and asked them to lead a section of the prayers. The BBC caught wind of it and publicised it on every radio station multiple times that day. 48 hours after the riots we held a prayer meeting for over a thousand with leaders of all the faith communities in Ealing and the deputy mayor of London. My church did the funeral for the man who had been murdered in the riots and I represented the diocese of London in the post riot analysis with the deputy mayor. It was quite overwhelming but amazing to see what could be done with the help of networks like social media. A year later a local newspaper asked if I had a message for Ealing. I said that I thought it was time we forgave the rioters. I wasn't expecting this to be such radical statement "Vicar suggests that community forgives" but a journalist in the Telegraph wrote an article about how terrible I was for daring to suggest it at all.

THE MEDIA

My first serious television appearance was half way through my curacy. A friend found herself unwell hours before doing a 5 minute newspaper review on Saturday morning breakfast show on Sky News. The other guest was John McCririck: racing commentator, mutton-chop sporting and outrageous sexist television persona (he only seems to refer to his wife as "The Boobie"). So they wanted a feisty woman who could respond to any comments he said on air and avoid thousands of complaint emails flooding in. I had no idea what to do but I had a lot of media people in my church and I'm always trying to find out more about people's Monday to Friday contexts, so it sounded like a fun one off experience. I really didn't know what I was doing. I picked all the wrong stories! John was surprisingly kind in the Green Room helping me to find my way through. On air he didn't say anything about women, but he did heavily insult Liverpool, which is where I'm from. He was suitably outrageous and I nearly stabbed him with a pen. It made quite good viewing. They got a lot of tweets in about this young, female vicar so decided to invite me back regularly.

Due to the fact that I was on Sky News once a month or so, I got noticed by other groups. The Telegraph, the Independent, the Evening Standard, and Morrison's Magazine called when they needed a parish priest to quote. I continue to do quite a lot of television and radio, and I'm currently doing a lot with BBC Breakfast. My background in Oxford thinking of ways to answer difficult questions about faith came to the fore and it's a privilege to have a platform to talk about God with people who wouldn't normally listen to preachers and priests. We filled two Alpha Courses at my church with people who had looked me up online because they had seen me on television and felt they could trust me to explore faith with them and I had (and still do have) many, many conversations with people on the underground or in the street every time I go on television. It's mostly young women who come up to me:

"Sorry to stare, I saw you on the BBC this morning."

"Oh really. So what did you think about the issue?"

"I thought it was..." and they start talking about God or the church or ethics. Then being kind or maybe just polite they normally follow it with "I'm not really religious but I thought you made some good points." To which I respond "Oh that's interesting, why aren't you religious?"

Working with the media it's easy to get sucked into their values. It's an all or nothing business where people's very souls depend on being more famous than the next person. I've been very aware that I'm in this world as a priest so I'm to bring the perspective of God with me in how I act and interact.

I quickly established a few rules that I hold most of the time when I deal with the press:

I prioritise most individual pastoral commitments and church commitments over media. I wouldn't have anything to say if I wasn't also a regular priest and I think it says something to the industry (and to myself) if I commit to prioritising Mrs Jones's visit to talk about the funeral of her late husband over being on Channel 4 News.

I try to give away as many opportunities as I take. I've often given away opportunities that I can do because I knew I could put forward someone who I think would be another good voice in the press. One of the things I'm most proud about from the amount I've done in the press is that it's opened doors for a range of Christian women to be heard. The world doesn't need to know that there are young female priests wearing leather jackets, it needs to hear that there are a variety of voices in the church and, more to the point, that God is interested in everyone, not just "churchy types". It's also always a surprise (and I hope a thought provoking one) to the producer or researcher who calls me when I say "Well I could do the show but I think you'd be better with someone in inner-city ministry/hospital chaplaincy/more experience of men's ministry/etc".

I look for opportunities to highlight examples of as many everyday churches doing great things or small things with great love as I can.

I've never approached newspapers or television shows to have me on. Not once. I wouldn't even know how to do that. The call comes in and I have to decide if it's right for me to take.

I suppose the big media moment was over the women bishops debate. BBC Breakfast had asked me to go on to outline the discussion so I arrived at General Synod a bit late and in full television make-up. Surprisingly there was still plenty of room in the viewing gallery with just female priests and a few supporters sending up silent prayers. It filled up through the morning as the debate progressed. At lunchtime we had to line up outside again to get tickets for the afternoon's discussion. We were sitting ducks for the press and the paparazzi flashes started almost as soon as we lined up. I think it was because I was in TV make up or perhaps it was that I was in my everyday leather jacket that I ended up as one of those they focused on. I suppose it tied into their message of the young world vs. the old order.

THE (FAKE) LEATHER JACKET

As part of my theology of chaplaincy I dress in similar clothes to what I would wear if I was doing whatever I do not do as a priest. I wear skinny jeans for casual work and an office dress for formal and just slip in my clerical collar. I feel it symbolizes the part of but different role I have as a chaplain. Many chaplains (including myself) often get sucked into either being so different from those they work with that they have no connection, or being so similar that they have nothing to offer to the discussion. To make a difference you have to be different, but it's never an easy part. I'm not like a 'resident alien', building my own Christian subculture oasis while surrounded by the prevailing secular culture or like third generation immigrants who have no difference from their adopted culture. Christians, and in particular Anglican chaplains, are best summed up by the metaphor of rebirth. We are not outsiders come to fix the culture, but people of the culture: born and raised in it but then reborn into Christ who is already there and with the culture experiencing the resurrecting power of God's love. This is particularly important to me as a woman priest on the younger end of the spectrum.

I come into contact with so many young girls and women who feel that the church is not for them. Young women are one of the fastest rising groups to drop out of church attendance in the UK and the least likely to put themselves forward for ordination. As someone who has worked with youth, students and young professionals for over 10 years I feel strongly that one of the contributing factors to this is the lack of role models. It's amazing how quickly people's perceptions change when they just meet a young woman they can relate to who takes faith seriously and isn't embarrassed about that.

A week before the women bishops vote I did an interview and photo shoot with a London women's magazine about my daily life as a university chaplain. I packed a formal suit jacket for the shoot but had come from meeting students so was wearing my less formal leather one from Topshop. The photographer asked if she could take a few shots of me in the jacket after the formal shoot as it was quite a contrast with my collar. We didn't think they'd use it as it wasn't the look they'd asked for but she thought it was an interesting contrast. It's the type of thing I wear most days so I was happy to oblige. To our surprise the magazine loved it and used that shot as well as one of me in formal robes.

On the day of the women bishops debate I was surprised how much coverage that fake leather jacket got around the world. After the debate there followed a deluge of media inquires. I turned down almost everything. I'd done a lot of media work, maybe fifty television and radio appearances over the past two years. I had an opportunity to speak out at a time when the world was calling the church, and calling God, sexist. With the help of the Church Communications team I picked through the list of calls. The Times called and asked if I'd do an interview and photo shoot for their women's magazine. A string of news programs had me on and it was all going well. Along with the other people speaking in the press, we seemed to be changing the culture from thinking we were the victims of a sexist institution to thinking we were part of an empowering faith and trying to work towards showing this in the church. It was going well.

The Evening Standard wanted to do the same style of shoot that had been in Stylist magazine the week before. Both the communications team and I were happy with the photographs that came out from that. I turned up in knee high flat boots but didn't see the harm in agreeing to put on a pair of heels as that was the look I'd done the previous week. My stomach turned when pictures came out. My heels looked a lot higher than I thought they were and the same dress I wore in the Stylist Magazine shoot looked a lot shorter in the second shoot. It was quite a learning curve about how much difference lighting and camera angle can make.

I was also surprised that week how much print media misquote you. At best the things you read as quotes are the journalist's summary of what they heard you say over an hour's interview. My media mentor told me that even if everything you say is perfect, even if you speak in sound bites that you don't mind being taken out of context, even if you check and recheck the quotations and photographs they intend to use, you will still be misquoted 10% of the time and only 20% of what you really want to say will get through their filter of their perspective on the story. But it's normally worth doing it for the 20% of message you get through to people who wouldn't hear it otherwise.

Being in the media as a priest involves making the same type of decisions I have to make as a chaplain but with the world watching. As a chaplain you have to make controversial decisions all the time. Do you travel across London with a friendless student who is going to have an abortion if you are worried she might not get home safely? Do you let the Wicca society use the multi-faith chaplaincy building that you manage? Do you sit with a student who is having their 6th drink in the bar? Good chaplains can't run on ethical autopilot. It's one of the things I love about it. There is always the question of "What does it really mean to be the Good News of Christ in this situation?" Always.

I've often been struck by the writings of Dietrich Bonhoeffer on ethics. It's easy to stand back and maintain personal distance from the messy situations of life but it's rarely the most loving response and it may actually be a selfish response. Dietrich Bonhoeffer managed to get safe passage to New York and London away from his home in 1930s Germany and the Nazis. But he took the last boat home convicted that his personal holiness and distinctiveness from the evil that was gripping his homeland was a luxury that the followers of Christ didn't have. We do the best we can and then we throw ourselves on the mercy of God. I'm convinced that when we humbly try to follow Christ, God uses us. We do the best we can and we throw ourselves on the mercy of God.

I had been warned by my media mentor and the church communications team that I would get a lot of criticism for the amount I was in the press over the woman bishops debate. I only did 2 newspaper interviews that week in the end, the Times and the Evening Standard. It was unnerving to have unwanted attention from reporters and photographers and articles written as if they had spoken to me directly. I was warned that my phone might be tapped and my bins gone through. A friend came to stay and overheard me being woken at 3am by the producer of a news program I'd become friends with calling to warn me that the Daily Mail had run a nasty piece on me. I then spent an hour on the phone to someone from the London diocese 24hour communications helpline who mercifully got out of bed to help me work out what to do.

I was surprised as many people within the church were supportive. There was a twitter support campaign, and a lot of emails and messages from friends and strangers who saw through the media manipulation. I was very grateful to receive the concerned emails as well. Without exception people wrote back to say they felt reassured once I'd had an opportunity to tell them about the context. I wanted to communicate that God cares about young women at a time when all the headlines were effectively saying that the church didn't. And I think I succeeded. A lot of media people have said how they realised how diverse the church is. I've had over a thousand emails and tweets from women who never go to church asking for advice on exploring God or just saying that they were struck by how they could imagine themselves going to church now. Thousands of vicars are doing a great job around the UK talking about Jesus in ways that make sense in their surroundings. I hope my work in the media makes people more likely to go to their local church and see that. But my ultimate aim is to promote Christ, even more than promoting the church so I hope the biggest legacy of me being a more public priest is that people engage with God.

But I'd had my fill by then. I was being called to go on all sorts of television programs but decided to turn everything down for the month leading up to Christmas. I wanted time to take stock, and I needed to get back to my day job. I try to remember that the only sure thing about being flavour of the month is that you won't be flavour of next month. And that this is okay. We are doing this as a whole church!

The media is a ruthless industry and exhausting as well as exhilarating for those who depend on it. As a priest in the media, it's important to build a new framework for engagement, one that is based on God's peace and the Sermon on the Mount. I've never been more grateful for the security of my close friends and family and for the love of God than in my work in the media. But the routine of life, of daily bible reading and prayer, of talking to my family on the phone and getting back to regular parish life keeps me as a priest rather than a celebrity. I was talking to the Reverend Rose Hudson Wilkin last week. Rose is the chaplain to the Houses of Parliament and was just about to dash in to support an MP facing a scandal. She said "I will then come back and go to a local school for the small A-level art show of someone in my church, I couldn't miss it, I've encouraged her to do it! And no one else I'll meet in Westminster has the range of experiences we do every day". In the early days I'd think about the context I was working in, the fact that I'd jump from a toddler's playgroup to a news studio to a nursing home to being alone in my study writing a sermon. I found it unsettling and unnerving until one day I realised it wasn't about the setting, it wasn't even really about me: it's about the message; it's about God's love. All I can do is be ready to talk about that in any context I'm offered.

For me, chaplaincy is as much about my media work as it is about my university work; as much about Facebook as it is about walking the streets of my parish. It's a way of thinking, a belief that the line between sacred and secular is not the wall of the church, but runs down every human heart. It's the solid hope that God, because of the incarnation, is already at work, bringing the world to his resurrected life, and our challenge as Anglican Chaplains (but no less so as Christians) is to spot that, celebrate it, and join in!

Allowing God's voice to lead

Clare Hendry

Looking back over my life so far it seems to be one with no obvious logical path through, no careful career development. I think if I had told my friends at school that I would be ordained into the Church of England and that I would spend a large part of my working life teaching in theological colleges they would have laughed. A similar reaction might have been found amongst my friends at University, even the ones in the Christian Union with me – where to make sure I came to the individual college prayer meetings they would sometimes hold them in my room! God is full of surprises!

One of the things I love about ministry—both as a lay and ordained person—is the variety of things it has given me an opportunity to do. And although at one level there hasn't been a careful progression through, as I look back, I can see how God has woven the different things I have done into his purposes for my life.

I went off to university to do a degree in Religious Studies followed by a PGCE (Post graduate certificate of education) and began to teach RE in London whilst living in Cambridge. I was involved in a local church, helped set up an art and music festival in Ely—life was good and ordination not even on the horizon, but then things took a change in direction. So that a couple of years later I was on a plane heading to Jackson, Mississippi. I was about to start a two year Masters in Marriage and Family Therapy at Reformed Theological Seminary. They were two of the most significant years in my life. Being ordained in the Church of England, however, was still not part of the plan – at least not part of my plan.

There were ups and downs over those two years but I am so grateful to God for leading me there and for the friends who had first introduced me to RTS and helped make it possible for me to study there. It was there that I first began to look at what the bible taught about the role of women. Before that I hadn't even realised that there were different views! At some stage during my time there, and I really can't remember when or how, I gradually felt a calling to work not only in the area of counselling, but for some strange reason, to work in the Church of England. The call felt rather vague but very real. I wasn't sure quite what the next step was but, being ever the pragmatist, I knew that if I was going to follow that calling I needed to have some means to live by. Ordination seemed the most obvious pathway. I wasn't aware of any other way of fulfilling what I felt God was calling me to. So eighteen months after heading to Mississippi I was back on a plane flying to the UK to see a DDO (Diocesan Director of Ordinands) and my home church vicar to begin exploring the possibility of ordination, or so I thought. I finished my Masters in the States and once again headed back to the UK and to a selection conference for ordination. Now I could follow my calling to work in the Church of England.

Just one slight blip – well actually quite a major one! I wasn't recommended. Had I heard right from God? Maybe He meant me to do something else? I had a very encouraging bishop, who seemed, like me, slightly bemused as to the reasons stated for not recommending me. He encouraged me not to rule it out for ever but to think about it again at some later date.

Great, so what next? Back home with no obvious open door. Eventually I ended up back in Cambridge working as an administrator in the NHS in the local mental hospital. But was that really where God wanted me to serve him—in administration? Was that really what I had spent two years training for in Marriage and Family Therapy? What of the call I had heard – or had I misheard?

One of the things I learnt, and see even more clearly as I look back, is how we need to trust in God's plans for us. He can see the big picture and he knows where he wants us. Which is why, a year after not being recommended for Ordination training, I drove into the grounds of Oak Hill Theological College (an Anglican theological college) to begin work as the new lecturer in Pastoral Counselling. Who says God hasn't got a sense of humour!

Perfect, now I understand—counselling and the Church of England—not quite in the package I had envisaged but actually I think probably a better package for me. Indeed although not ordained until several years later I count this as the beginning of my ministry. What was incredible was that the kind of things the college was ideally looking for in this appointment was actually quite an odd mix. They wanted a person who could teach Pastoral Counselling (clear tick there) and if you could do a bit of World Religions that would be useful (a degree in Religious Studies and two years as an RE teacher) and oh there is a need for someone to help with Admissions (administration experience helpful – thank you NHS!). Any experience of working with people from other churchmanship? That would be useful for teaching on the part-time ordination courses run then by Oak Hill, which drew students from across the breadth of the Church of England. Well having one of my referees as the Chaplain at the hospital, with whom I had worked quite closely, and who was of a different churchmanship from me, didn't harm my application.

My side trip into working for the NHS, which at some stages seemed like a bit of a distraction, was in fact very much part of God's plan in equipping me for what he was calling me into. I hope that this is a real encouragement for those who sometimes feel that what they are doing or are involved in is not useful. God knows what lies ahead for us and he uses all things in our lives to achieve his purpose for his people.

The next few years were a steep learning curve in many ways. I knew very little about the Church of England and its organisation and yet here I was training people to become part of it.

Along with the other tutors at Oak Hill I also taught on our part-time ministerial training course.

That was an interesting experience with ups and downs. It was the place where I think I first really became aware of the breadth of the Church of England. The staff teaching on the course, at the time, were evangelicals but the students came from a diverse range of theological backgrounds and on the whole were older than the full time students – all a bit daunting for a woman in her late twenties – younger than most of the students on the part-time course and with little background in the Church of England. It was good preparation for later years and stood me in good stead for being part of a Chapter where there is a diversity of churchmanship which on the whole I have come to appreciate. What I found fascinating on the course was how much in common some of the students from Anglo-Catholic backgrounds had with their fellow evangelical students.

In time I took on the role of senior tutor on the part-time course, working closely with the vice-Principal, David Field, who ran the course under the Principal. It was a great experience and I learnt a lot working alongside him. I quickly discovered more about the way the Church of England works, which was a good thing as I ended up basically running the course when David took a sabbatical. This involved working with representatives from both London and

St Albans's dioceses, who were on the management team for the course.

Alongside this I was teaching pastoral counselling on the full-time course and over the years enjoyed developing the modules I had inherited and creating new ones. I did do some teaching in the area of World Religions. For a time I was involved with Admissions and even planning some of the publicity, not one of my strong points but I guess in ministry we are often called to do some things which are not always playing to our strengths but still need doing. I was involved in being a fellowship tutor to a group of around 10 students who I was with throughout their time at college

Whilst I had the academic qualifications for teaching pastoral counselling I still needed to gain further experience in the practice. I was fortunate to be able to join a counselling group based down at the International Presbyterian Church, where I not only did some counselling but also go involved with the Association of Biblical Counsellors and helped with some of their short courses they ran. Through this I met my husband – no not a counsellor or clergyman but an ex-Brethren consulting engineer from Scotland.

After four years I had another 'addition' to my family in the shape of our first child Kate. I was really fortunate that I could carry on working at Oak Hill but on a part-time basis. We were blessed by great child-minders on campus in the shape of the wives of some of the students. I could also work more in the term-time especially when both children were at school and thus have more time off in the holidays which worked really well as the children grew (four years after Kate, Alistair had joined and completed the family). I loved being able to spend some time at home looking after the children but also being able to carry on in ministry.

I hope that as more women are being ordained into full-time stipendiary ministry, many of whom are mothers, it will challenge the Church of England to think about how ministry works with a family—this needs to apply for men as well. Ministry can bring a great blessing in that, although it has its challenges for family life, it has a flexibility that many other jobs don't offer. I think I made all my children's sports days and most of their class assemblies with the odd school trip thrown in as well.

Over the years at Oak Hill I had the opportunity to help with the American programme where we had students coming over from the USA to spend a semester with us. I did some outside speaking at various churches, many invitations coming through contacts from Oak Hill. One invitation involved a trip to St Andrews, the Anglican Church in Moscow, spending a weekend teaching on pastoral care in the church and then preaching on Sunday, where the congregation included an agent from the FSB (Russian secret police). I did a bit of teaching at London School of Theology on family therapy and also taught a module for two years at Kings' College London on their MA in Youth Ministry. What I loved about working at Oak Hill was the variety of things I was involved in over the time I was there and the many people I met there.

But in the middle of my time at Oak Hill God threw in another challenge. A year or so after Kate was born there I was teaching at Oak Hill and married with one child. I had also started a doctor of ministry programme at Westminster Theological seminary in Philadelphia, a few years before Kate was born. This involved in going over to the States to do some short intensive courses in counselling which was great. I was able to spend part of a sabbatical there working on my thesis proposal as well as sitting in on some of the counselling courses for their equivalent of ordinands. After several years at Oak Hill this was really helpful in reviewing what I was teaching and in developing some of my courses. I was now working on my thesis as well as being a Mum and working so time was rather limited. I had more than enough on my plate or so I thought. God, as usual, had different plans for me.

The thought of being ordained came up again. A few people over the years had mentioned it and to be honest I can't quite remember how it cropped up. I know that part of it came from a pragmatic reason. We had a Bishops' inspection of the college, something which all Anglican theological training colleges and courses have every five years or so. One of the criticisms in the report was that Oak Hill only had one ordained woman on staff. In fact I think at that time, certainly amongst colleges, we had more women on staff than many did, just not all of them were ordained. So I think partly the reason for revisiting the possibility of ordination was it would help Oak Hill to have another ordained female member of staff and also at some stage if I ever left Oak Hill, something I wasn't planning to do in the near future, I would like to work in a local church. Having some kind of recognition of a calling by the wider Church of England might help. But pragmatism apart, God was also clearly calling me down this track and now was His time for it to happen.

So I ended up going to see the DDO (Diocesan Director of Ordinands) who I had worked with in the management team of the part-time course. The area of London diocese that I was in was strongly Anglo-Catholic and didn't exactly have a strong reputation of being in favour of or always very supportive of women in ministry. The time was just after women had been admitted to the priesthood and so in many ways a difficult time for some of the Anglo-Catholic clergy. I wasn't sure what response I would get but I have to say that my experience was very positive as from the moment I first saw my DDO he could not have been more supportive and indeed seemed surprised that I hadn't come forward before. My experience with the bishop also was very supportive. My first degree and subsequent MA had covered much of what ordinands did at Oak Hill and so the bishop graciously said that in my training I should just fill in the gaps and so that was what I did. Spending some time on one side of the desk and then swapping to the other to be taught by my colleagues was a slightly surrealistic experience!

I was licensed to my home church of St James, Muswell Hill as honorary curate. It was great to get some experience in the parish, although this was limited because of work and family. I had chosen to go for the permanent deaconate because I had some questions over headship and the role of women in ministry. In my studies back at seminary and over the following years I had dipped in and out of looking at what I felt the bible was teaching about women and ministry and felt convinced about male headship (to see why and how I got there you will need to read Lis Goddard's and my book on women in ministry—The Gender Agenda [IVP]—more about this a bit later)

I loved my time at Oak Hill and one of the things I still enjoy is seeing former students at various events and hearing what they are doing and seeing how God is working through them in many settings. It was a great privilege to be involved in some of their training and to develop some good friendships.

I find it strange and to be honest a bit sad when some people on hearing I had been on the staff at Oak Hill look pitying at me and say 'didn't you find that hard being a woman?', therefore implying that Oak Hill was in some way anti-women, which was not the case. No, not at all, I had brilliant colleagues who were very supportive. David Peterson, one of the Principals I worked with was a great encourager when I first started preaching in college chapel. Yes a lot of the staff, but not all, believed in male-headship but then so did I, which is why I went for the permanent diaconate. I do, however, think that it is quite possible for a woman to be priested and still hold to male headship within the church. When women were allowed to be priested, the college was committed to the two integrities and we had men and women training for ministry from both integrities.

So what next? Well I was fairly settled at Oak Hill and enjoying family life with two children and some involvement at St James but then out of the blue I was made redundant—surely that doesn't happen at a theological college! Alas it does but I had an incredible sense of God's peace, although it was not easy to leave a place which had been such an important part of my and my family's life. But God is good and He had prepared ahead. We had sold our house in Cambridge a few years earlier and bought one nearby which we had rented out so we had somewhere to go. I was asked to carry on teaching my modules but as a visiting lecturer, which I was happy to do. I was then also asked by my vicar to join the paid staff at St James as Minister for Pastoral Care. God had already prepared what I was to do next.

After two years of juggling a young family, lecturing and working at St James, along with being involved with various organisations like Fellowship Word and Spirit, I thought something had to go so somewhat reluctantly I called it a day on teaching at Oak Hill. Over the next few years I got stuck into pastoral work at St James. Some of this involved one to one work and I was able to use a lot of my counselling training in this area. I also ran short courses on pastoral care helping to equip others to be involved in pastoral work.

Steve and I had been there as members of the congregation since just after we were married and so we had been around at St James for a while. It was great working with the team there and again a privilege seeing over the years how God was at work in the lives of the people there. I did miss teaching the students but there were opportunities to do some teaching in the church and I appreciated the opportunity to do more one to one work, not just in the area of counselling, but also discipling. I was part of the senior staff team and I learnt so much about ministry from my colleagues especially from my vicar, Alex Ross – a brilliant leader with a strong servant-heart. It was great to be involved in a leadership team but in a way that I felt comfortable with from a theological viewpoint. Again as at Oak Hill there have been various opportunities to do lots of things including getting more involved with the women's work and starting up the Women's Weekend Away.

Being part-time and a SSM (Self-Supporting Minister) and rather a specialist I feel that instead of getting more specialised over the years I have almost done the opposite. When I first started at St James I was very much working in the pastoral care and counselling side and I had done very little of the bread and butter things that a 'normal' curate would have done. There were still gaps in my experience which at some stage might need filling.

I began to get some opportunities to do a bit of teaching at Wycliffe Hall in Oxford and was then asked to join their Hall Council. So I now get a chance to make regular journeys over to Wycliffe to teach and also contribute through the work of the Council drawing on my parish as well as college experience.

I guess the next big thing that I got involved with was writing a book. Now at the back of my mind I thought I might write a book one day in the area of pastoral care and counselling but this was a book in women and ministry! I had met Lis Goddard at NEAC where the idea for a group supporting ordained evangelical women in the Church of England came out of, now known as AWESOME. Through my involvement with AWESOME I got to know Lis. One evening she emailed me to see if I would like to work with her on a book about women's ministry. The idea was for two ordained Anglican women, who both hold a high view of Scripture, but disagree on the role of women in ministry, to explore together what the Bible says and to talk about why they hold the position they do. In a moment of insanity I said yes! It was so out of my comfort zone but I thought it was a really important thing to do. In my time at Oak Hill obviously the whole debate about women and ministry had cropped up many times. I had first begun to think about it myself when writing an essay back in seminary on certain passages about women in Corinthians. I also had been forced to think about what I felt I was being called to do when I went forward for ordination. In some ways being what was then called a non-stipendiary minister meant it was easier to find a role where I didn't ever feel pressure to take the next step and become a vicar. Lis and I shared the same conviction, not about the role of women in the church, but the need to properly engage with each other, to listen to each other and to encourage others to do that as well. Even more crucial we were committed to exploring together the bible to see what it had to say. I have come across so many people, from both sides, who hold strong views on women's ministry but who have never really engaged with the texts and have assumed they know what the 'other side' thought and often had written them off. So then started the emails as we worked through the main texts—oh what joy it was when the send button was pressed! Until the next email from Lis arrived and the pressure was on. Finally it was finished! The response to it has been encouraging but also slightly worrying in that the main thing reviewers and others have commented on was how gracious we were to each other as we disagreed. We get the same comments when we go and speak to churches and theological colleges about women in ministry. I found that a bit shocking! Lis is my sister in Christ and we may disagree on things, but whilst it is an important issue it is not a salvation issue. Surely we should be able to find a way to work together for the sake of gospel as indeed we have.

Over two years ago I decided that the time was right to move on from St James. At some stage Steve and I hope to escape from London and want to serve and get involved in a local church, which is unlikely to be the size of St James. We thought it might be a good idea to get some experience of being part of a smaller church. So off to see the bishop to see what could be next. The reality though was that in our area is that there wasn't much available for a SSM permanent deacon, who because of schools couldn't move for the next few years. There was certainly lots of work to be done but not the funding to go with it. But as ever God had the place and a place where for various reasons I had thought wasn't a possibility – the church plant from St James which had been planted into pub about 8 years ago. So here I am at Grace Church on the edge of Muswell Hill, as honorary assistant minister. No longer in the pub but borrowing space in two different churches for our morning and afternoon service. It's been great to renew friendships with people who had been part of the original plant and to get to know new folk. I decided that I needed to fill in some of the gaps which I might have covered if I had gone the normal curate training route like helping with primary school children – again out of my comfort zone. But for the last two years or so I have been involved in helping with an after school club learning from others and I must admit really enjoy going and getting alongside the children. They haven't got me teaching in Sunday school yet but who knows what lies ahead!

There are many challenges for us as a church of not having a permanent home other than the vicarage, especially as we grow in numbers and want to reach out into the community but God is gracious and will provide in His way and His timing. We just need to keep trusting and praying. We are very aware that we don't want to get so distracted in trying to find a permanent home that we neglect what God has called us to do in reaching out to the Community with the Gospel. I have learnt so much about ministry working alongside the team lead by Philip, the vicar. And I am continuing to learn more and more about God's grace and provision for me as an individual and for us as a church.

As I look ahead I don't know what lies in the future for me in ministry. If I think back to arriving at Oak Hill and starting all those years ahead I would never have predicted I would be where I am now and having done what I have done. I still feel called to work in the Church of England and hope there will be a place for me, as someone who believes in male headship but feels able to work in a church, where with proper provision, I along with others can work with those who hold a different view for the sake of the Gospel. The Church of England has many challenges ahead both internally and externally. My concern is that as the Church tries to work a way forward on women bishops that there won't be a place for many of our Anglo-Catholic brethren or the more conservative evangelicals who hold to male headship. There are so many other challenges for the

Gospel that we need to hold together and learn how to be involved in furthering God's kingdom for his glory.

What lies in the future? For the Church of England there are many challenges that lie ahead. All we can do is pray for the Church that it would remain faithful to the Gospel and keep encouraging men and women to serve, through the Church of England, whether as clergy or laity.

For me personally? I have no idea, but my heavenly Father does. Being a permanent deacon can restrict, on one level, opportunities to work in churches, especially if you are looking for a salary. It can be a role that is sometimes marginalised. Some people can view you as somehow a second class citizen in relation to the 'real' ordained but we are all the priesthood of believers and all have a part to play in God's kingdom. As a permanent deacon I have been able to use the gifts God has given me in a variety of settings.

So I am looking forward to the future not sure quite what it will hold but knowing that God has planned it and that's all I need to know.

The voice of hope

Jane Morris

I became a Christian during my last year at school in London in the late 60s. Through the witness of a Christian friend from a local Methodist Church, I started to pray, read the New Testament and go to a local church. But it was not until I went to University in York that I met Christians who were talking about some of the inner experience of God in which I was growing. For several years, I attended both a lively Methodist Church in York as well as St Cuthbert's Church—where David Watson was the Curate in charge. So for several years I lived a bit of a double life—something that has probably laid foundations for the way God has led me in the years that followed.

In the mornings I would go to Centenary Methodist Church—and I read enthusiastically all the books by W E Sangster—a great Methodist preacher and inspiring leader. And in the evenings I would go along to St Cuthbert's—where there was great teaching, an open approach to the charismatic renewal and the very beginnings of the way in which many have come to express sung worship. The Thursday evening fellowship meetings at the Rectory were such a formative highlight for me—week by week there was bible teaching from David Watson, and a 'part 2' of the evening where groups spread throughout the house would pray and seek God, and grow in all sorts of spiritual gifts.

The Methodist students used to go out in 'preaching teams' to the various town and country churches in the circuit, and I joined these with enthusiasm. Through this connection, I was also privileged to attend Cliff College for the Derwent Convention several times. There were a couple of occasions at this event where something like revival broke out—which left a fairly permanent impression on me. It was also at this event that I first encountered the ministry of the Holy Spirit in a more personal way, through which I received and grew in some of the gifts of the Holy Spirit. As this developed, I sensed God calling me to offer as a Methodist Local Preacher—a foundation for which I have been very grateful— coming as it did with a very thorough grounding in learning to preach.

In my parallel church life at St Cuthbert's, God was at work in all sorts of exciting ways that have reverberated into the wider life of the church in all sorts of ways in subsequent years. Teams from the church would travel with David Watson in various missions across the nation and the world. I was growing in my Christian life, voraciously reading all sorts of books, learning to pray—and we were seeing God at work in wonderful ways. In my final year at University, I lived in the Rectory with David and Anne Watson and their children as the 'student in the attic'—a little before it became a larger community—and again here I learned and grew.

Towards the end of my time at University, it became clear that I needed to belong to one church rather than attending two—and certainly my heart and friends were in St Cuthbert's—so that was the choice. It did, however, come at the cost of stopping my Local Preacher ministry. I can remember a conversation with David Watson where he said that he thought that a woman should not be preaching and teaching in church—something that was the general view in Anglican evangelical churches. I was somewhat confused by this, as I had a strong inner call and love of this ministry—but at the same time a respect for those from whom I had learned so much. I reluctantly came to the conclusion that perhaps they knew more than me and that I might have got it wrong.

By that time, I had then bought a house in York, and was teaching science and chemistry. That was at a time when as a single woman, it was reasonably unheard of that you could get a mortgage to buy your own property! York City Council were very go-ahead for the time, and I was able to get a 'Council Mortgage' from them, provided that my father acted as a male guarantor. I mention this since we sometimes forget how far a journey we have come. This was a time when you would look at the TV and say—'look, there is a woman reading the news!' And similarly in our evangelical church, women could read the lesson in services occasionally—and we would think—'look, there is a woman reading the bible!' As a single woman it was a layer harder, since women mostly had roles in church as an extension of the ministry of their husbands.

Over the following years, there was some contention in our church as in many others over the role of women in the life and ministry of the church— and some left for pastures new because of this. This did mean that there was a slightly greater freedom for women to grow into a greater range of ministries. And so over a number of years I was involved in all sorts of ministries. I helped lead our youth ministry for some years, and then was particularly involved in evangelism and outreach. We would hold 'renewal weeks' at the church, where we welcomed numbers of visitors, and we continued to take teams overseas. I remember a particular time when I was part of a team visiting Sweden, and one evening where I particularly felt called back into a preaching and teaching ministry. Since I had previously been a Methodist Local Preacher, it was relatively simple to transfer this across to be an Anglican Lay Reader. This was welcomed within what was by then St Michael le Belfrey Church. Whilst I was the first female Lay Reader in the long history of the church—it was more that I was 'our Jane' and that God's call was recognised and welcomed by others.

In time this calling grew into a vocation to ordained ministry—but this proved somewhat hard to take forward, since those around me in the church were not quite sure what to do with me. I tried over some seven or eight years to push open this door, over which time the vision somewhat died within me. But with some new people in the wider diocese I gave it one more try, and doors started to open and I was recommended for training for ordained ministry.

During this time, I got to know a number of women in ministry, who had come through the route of 'lady worker' and deaconess. I did a placement in a church where the first woman to conduct a marriage service in the Church of England was on the staff. I remember the press contacting her and wanting to know if she was going to have her hair done for the occasion— surely a damned-if-you-do-damned-if-you-don't sort of question! I was struck by how hard it was for some of those wonderful women. Since women could not be ordained priest, then they could not lead a local church as vicar. So a number had male contemporaries who had gone forward into all sorts of exciting and fulfilling roles in ministry and leadership. But the role of a woman in ordained ministry was held back as that of an ongoing curate. It was a hard challenge to live with grace, but I got to know some inspiring women in ministry who helped and encouraged me along the way.

The decision by General Synod to enable women to be ordained to the priesthood came at just the time that enabled me to be ordained priest at the end of my year as a deacon. So I joined with the first women who gathered in York Minster to be ordained priest. I remember we held our breath when it came to the bit where someone could raise an objection, and how the legal beagles all robed up in the cathedral were somewhat crestfallen that they could not step in at such a dramatic point. In fact the only protest was a supportive group of Roman Catholics who were looking to see the same happen in their neck of the woods. And then the privilege of celebrating communion in both of our historic Church buildings— St Michael le Belfrey in the shadow of York Minster and the historic St Cuthbert's Church.

Over the next few years, I led one of the congregations at St Michael's and continued to grow and love ministry in the local church. I also came to the decision that I felt it right to leave teaching (which I had continued to do for a while) and move into full time stipendiary ministry. When I left this long and wonderful time in York we marked it with a great party that celebrated all the different things I have done over the years—in many ways it was a telling of the story of the church. Living within all these ministries in the church, and reflecting on the leadership styles and decisions of others equipped me for ministry in a very thorough way. The big joke at the party was that I had done almost every job in the life of the church, except that I had never made a banner! And so having duly made a banner in public at the party, I was sent on my way thoroughly equipped for ministry in the wider world.

When I left York, I moved to St George's Leeds where I was the Associate Minister for some ten years. I grew to love the people and local church ministry more and more, and I still have many good friends there. I learned and grew in understanding and the skills of growing and sustaining the life of a local church.

Whilst in Leeds I was also involved in the growing life of New Wine, which was an exciting and liberating way forward for me. As a good Evangelical Anglican Charismatic (we always used to have discussions as to what order you should put those words in...) I had been variously part of things like 'Come Together', the Fountain Trust, Lytchett Minster and more. But whilst I was receiving and growing in God, I was often in a quite painful position in such gatherings. I found most of the male leaders would relate in a man-to-man way with their friends, colleagues and often contacts from theological college. But they would unconsciously miss me, talking past me and over my head and mostly assuming I was someone else's wife that they did not know. And it was the beginnings of New Wine in the north of England that turned this around for me. Out of the years in York, God had done amazing things, and many of the church leaders across the north that I was meeting were already my friends, having had connections with us in York. And so I became 'me' and part of a network of leaders and no longer invisible. While I was in Leeds, I also started the West Yorkshire New Wine Network and we found it was so encouraging to meet with other like minded leaders across our region and to see what God was doing. It was also fun attending the national Network Leaders gatherings where at the time there were only two of us that were female—it was somewhat satisfying to attend a Christian event where the ladies could go straight into the loos at coffee time, whilst the men had to join a queue. Towards the end of my time in Leeds, I was also part of the leadership team that set up New Wine in the north, and I helped put in place all the teams that make the weeks of the Summer Conferences work.

I am grateful to God that he has hard wired a sense of humour over such things into my character. It might have been easy to grow grumpy and with a chip on the shoulder over the endless supply of comments, bias, assumptions—but happily I have been graced with a good supply of inner amusement. Going into a shop to buy something and they say 'is that Miss or

Mrs?'—to which one can answer—'Reverend' still amuses me—though it has happily nearly run out of its novelty value.

During the second half of my ten years in Leeds, I was seeking to see if I could move on to lead a church, and from time to time I would apply for various roles as an incumbent. It started to become quite a difficult journey, as most times I would be shortlisted for a final interview and then a man would be appointed to the job. I came to see that this was a bit of a transition time for women in evangelical Anglican churches. Amongst the first tranche of those of us ordained with the first women priests, only a minority came from an evangelical persuasion. And so there were not very many of us coming through to approach the role of incumbent. In addition to this, a fairly strong dynamic, that still continues, is that of the role of the Parish Representatives. These people that have an important say in the appointment of their new Parish Priest are in many ways the 'gatekeepers' to the appointment. They have been entrusted with this important role by their fellow church members—and so naturally they want to get it right and are cautious. For most of them, appointing a woman would be an unprecedented step that no-one had done before in their context. So there was a tension going on that happens at new beginnings, between the call of God on one hand and the caution with the new on the other.

I remember a vivid call from God that came whilst watching a wildlife programme about the life of penguins! At a particular time, the penguins would gather on the edge of the water in large numbers, but none would be first to jump into the perilous waters. Eventually, one would jump in, then two or three, then hundreds. And clear as a bell I sensed God saying 'I want you to be that first penguin'. Through necessity and temperament, I had always been in the role of second or third penguin. But that call to be first in the water, with all its excitement, risks and perils, has been a bit of a leadership theme that God has grown in my life.

Towards the end of my time in Leeds, I was able to take a three month sabbatical where I wanted to seek God's way forward. I travelled to London for a New Wine Leader's retreat in Harrow, and while I was there several people asked me if I knew that they were looking for a new vicar in St Gabriel's Cricklewood. I had not actually told anyone there I was wondering about a new job, and had never heard of this church. However in the way that God catches your attention by repeating himself, this job kept coming up in all sorts of ways during the week. And so it happened that I applied and was appointed. I think that the 'gatekeepers' and culture at St Gabriel's were such that prayer and being open to what God was saying and calling were at the forefront, rather than the fear of innovation. And so my present role as vicar of St Gabriel's began.

I do believe that God weaves patterns of calling and gifting into our lives, and I have seen several of these. Another version of 'first penguin' is something I have come to call 'Jane the Baptist' in that I have had a bit of a calling on my life to go into new places where often a woman has not been in that role before. And the challenge and call is to live and do it in such a way that it becomes normal, and then the next woman in that role after me just gets on with the job God has called her to. And the Church of Jesus Christ is the richer and more whole, as all the gifts and ministries that God has for his people are released for the Church and the World. I am often very aware of this dynamic when I step into new roles that perhaps a woman has not done before, and I believe my calling under God is to do it the best I can and in such a way that it becomes the norm.

In the early days of my being vicar of St Gabriel's, there were all sorts of new decisions and thoughts to grow into. Over so many years, it was easy to get into the way of thinking about what I would do if I was vicar, but without the responsibility of living with those decisions! Every ordained person starting their first vicar post experiences such a transition. But for me there was an additional layer in that there were few, if any, role models of women who were leading evangelical churches of any flavour. And so the question that I learned to ask myself was 'what does it mean to lead as me?' I could not keep up with the effort of being someone else, and in any case, it was me that God had called into this role.

I have always tried to be a lifelong student of church, and I remember being particularly struck by some of the findings of the Natural Church Development movement. One of the dynamics that makes churches healthy and therefore growing, is that leadership in the church should be empowering. Surveys within the UK showed that across our nation, this area often scored the lowest. I wondered about the largely male culture of leadership that many leaders had grown into when training for ordained ministry. So I thought a lot about how fast a local church community should travel. In the past I had seen some leaders who were so pioneering and Alpha-male-ish that they would run on ahead and call back to the strung out church community to 'Follow Me

Men!' And often the community would be so extended by this that some would leave for elsewhere or just get left behind. Equally church is called to be a pilgrim people on the move, led by God's Spirit—so I learned lessons about how leadership is often about recognising God at work and making room for that and joining in. About travelling at the pace that God is setting and seeking to bring the maximum number of people along who will come.

I tried to put into practice things that I had seen and learned about the church as God's community—and how we bring together both leadership and teamwork in a creative partnership, and how to enable us all to learn to listen to God and hear and heed what the Spirit is saying to the church, and then articulate that for the church. When we all hear God together, then more people will join in and come along as they share a united vision.

Being vicar of St Gabriel's was always and continues to be the main focus of my energies, my vision and passion for the local church. I really think I have the best job in the world, and feel privileged to be leading and equipping in the place of God's plan for the hope of the world. But throughout my ordained ministry, I have sought to 'tithe' my time by being open to be involved in two outside areas of ministry—

one within my own diocese and one on a more national level. I have found that balance to be both sustainable and inspiring—I have often wondered whether this is not a pattern that would be a great dynamic in the wider church. So whilst in Leeds I was at various times an examiner for an ordination course, on the Diocesan Ministerial Review team, on the New Wine in the North Leadership Team and leading the West Yorkshire New Wine Network. And although I tried to keep my head down when I moved to London, I was invited to join the London and the South East New Wine Leadership Team, and I was also invited into the role of the Area Advisor for the Healing Ministry. I have come to think that I have a calling into the role of being a 'leader of leaders' and this has had various outworkings in these and other ways.

In a similar balancing of inside/outside the local church, I have learned to get into a good balance between the life of the local church, and what I call 'away matches' where I have been invited to speak or teach at various outside wider events. I have adopted the pattern that I will not take on more than one away match each month and also where the outside event is a little more challenging, I will try to build in extra preparation time and not take on other invitations. Over time I and other female speakers have had the frustrating experience of frequently being invited to speak at events for women whilst at the same time hearing those seeking to fill preaching and teaching roles in national events lamenting the difficulty of finding 'a woman speaker'. I want to bless and encourage separate events for men and women—they have a particular value and inspiration. But at the same time my own particular heart and vision is for the church as a whole.

It has been enormously encouraging to see the journey forwards from the time when the first few women in the spotlight of speaking at larger events, where various ones either wanted them to be brilliant or to fail. There is still quite a journey to go in all this, but it is so good to see a growing number of women who are gracious and competent Christian leaders called into a whole diversity of roles and ministries and exercising the gifts God has given them for the blessing of the church of Jesus Christ.

Another area that I have come to learn about through all this is what I call the 'leadership mystique'. I think this is a particular hazard in a range of churches within an evangelical tradition. But I have also seen it in the 'Father-knows-best' in the life of some of my friends in a more catholic tradition. How do we learn to honour and respect leaders without putting them on impossible pedestals? It is one of the pitfalls of leadership roles that you can get to believe and live in the hype put around you, and forget you are a fellow-servant of Jesus called to be humbly walking with others in the way of the cross. It is a particular peril for women coming into leadership in the church that we pick up some of these less-Christ-like habits and attitudes that have been around—and it is good to pray for a humble heart, a sense of humour and insight into who we are called to be in Christ. One of the good things that will come out of all this is that as men and women are working alongside one another in leadership, the whole dynamic of Christ's church will be so much more whole and effective.

Several years ago now, this journey into new places took a fresh turn in that I sensed that God was calling me to stand for General Synod. This was not something to which I had given a great deal of thought, though I have to confess over quite a time I had been a bit of a nerd about church politics and what was going on in the wider life and conversations of the church. I used to read all the Synod documents online and listen to debates late into the night! I suppose all this started with the initial vote to ordain women to the priesthood. I had been part of the

Movement for the Ordination of Women (MOW) whilst in York and can vividly remember the knife-edge vote at that time. And somewhat wearily over time, I have followed all the successive commissions and debates about the role of women in the church. It was hard at times to hear that what I was doing and probably who I was, was an 'issue' or a 'problem'. I did not really think about the fact that I might actually get onto General Synod—particularly as London Diocese is a hotly contested place in these matters. But I did know that God had called me to stand, and so I did the best job I could about asking how to go about it, and asking people to vote for me—not something that came very naturally.

I can remember being rather amazed when I was actually elected onto Synod! And I took some little time to find out how it all worked—something I am still learning. I anticipate being on Synod for one five year term, but I would encourage others to consider being part of it for several five year terms, since the understanding of process and networks of relationships will make the whole membership of each individual more effective over time. I joined up with the Evangelical Group on General Synod ('EGGS')—which I found to be the largest group on the Synod. EGGS has a process to elect its executive committee, and various folk encouraged me to stand for this—which I did. Our committee has turned out to be a great group to be a part of—we differ in where we 'come from' within our evangelical heritage, but our membership can see themselves represented in the committee—and we have a good way of working together that is both visionary and strategic. Once I was settled in to membership of General Synod, I thought it was the right time to step down from leadership roles within New Wine—but I have remained in a role of being a contact point between New Wine and Synod.

I have naturally continued to follow, and now be part of, the protracted process to enable women to be bishops alongside men. I was seriously disappointed when the measure seeking to take this forward did not receive the necessary votes—although I understood how it happened and could see it coming only too clearly. I was a bit taken aback by how much grief this has brought in my own heart and that of others. It is one thing when what we do is criticised, but this process has been painful on an altogether deeper level, since it is to do with our very sense of call, vocation, and identity. I realise that others hold their views with equal depth—and all this trying so hard to make differing views travel together is not going to be quickly solved. For myself, I am now wondering about a simple and quite different way forward—and how God's Holy Spirit is going to lead us.

As a member of General Synod, I have made friends across umbrella groups with quite different perspectives. One thing I have felt strongly about in all this is that Christians above all people are called to be friends with one another, even in our disagreements. Sometimes it has been that in our frustrations, other people end up not talking or relating to others with whom they disagree. In the midst of all this, I have found myself growing friendships across an extraordinary range of people. And perhaps because I have not had a title or role in all this, then I have come to see a call of God to exercise influence. Sometimes in our structures we think that positions and titles are all important—and certainly we need men and women, called by God to serve alongside one another in all areas of the life of the church. But alongside this I have learned that friendship, conversations, linking people together, and making friends can often be the context in which the life of God's Spirit can breathe and all sorts of things can progress and bear fruit.

Whilst I thought I was on Synod with a view to play my small part in taking forward the role of women as bishops in the church, I have found myself much more taken up with issues around human sexuality—something that divides us in a much deeper way. In this and other areas where I have made all sorts of friendships, I have remained with an ongoing orthodox evangelical theology. And yet I have made good friends and been able to help initiate conversations between people of quite different convictions. I am not sure where God will take all this, but I feel that has been His call and leading in me, and my responsibility is to follow where God's Spirit is leading.

On a shelf at home I have a couple of Royal Doulton white china pieces of a mother and daughter. One was bought for me by my own mother and one I bought myself—and both at the time of my ordination. It has been an ongoing call on my life to be in the role of a mother in the church—and I suppose for me, this is at the heart of my vocation. Looking for new life in the family of God and seeking to nurture and grow that life. Seeing people on the brink of Christian faith and helping them come to a new birth is one of my greatest delights. Being in the beginnings of new areas of ministry and helping grow their DNA in the family likeness. Enabling people at all stages and ages of their Christian life to grow as disciples of

Jesus. Looking further afield and seeing the wider picture of all God is doing and how it all fits together and where we are going—these are some of the things that are life-giving for me.

In a parallel way, it has been a great privilege to help people seeking God's call into Christian ministry in various ways and encouraging them along the way. That has always been something going on, with a series of people alongside me, who hopefully I have encouraged and enabled along the way.

Learning the voice of prayer

Liz Hoare

The odds against me being ordained priest in the Anglican Church were strong. I was brought up in a lively Baptist church and was so involved in the music and youth work that I returned home at weekends from university to worship there. This kept me well insulated from Anglican churches until well into my second year. I studied history at Durham which I loved, though I had also loved RE at school and in fact found it an easier subject in which to do well. But folk at church were dubious about the merits of studying theology at university where I would be taught to question the Bible and might lose my faith. It didn't help when another member of the youth group did just that. So it was another ten years before I got to grips with biblical criticism and theologians of various persuasions. The Baptist church, however, gave me a love for the Bible and taught me that I could have a relationship with the living Lord Jesus and these remain the foundation of my Christian faith today.

I cannot remember not being a Christian. My parents had taken me along to church from the beginning. Sunday school was part of every Sunday and I grew up knowing that Jesus was my Saviour and friend. I was not baptised until I was fifteen which was the earliest age the Baptist church would allow, but I took communion from the age of eight. Even as a small child I loved the solemnity of communion and the choruses we sang as the bread and wine were distributed. It was a church that encouraged us to give our testimonies in public and so from a young age I practised articulating what being a Christian meant to me. As a very shy child, this was a very important thing to learn to do. There were two other important aspects of the Baptist church that influenced me. One was an emphasis on missionary work overseas. We had a number of members working abroad with missionary organisations and they were prayed for and mentioned often. The message I picked up was that it was a fine thing to be called to be a missionary but I was terrified that God might call me! Later on I was cross that he didn't seem to be calling me, despite having got to the place of being prepared to go if he did. Perhaps that was the point!

The other emphasis at church was the weekly prayer meeting. As with most churches it wasn't the best attended meeting of the week but it was probably the key to the way that God blessed that congregation. It lasted an hour and most of the time I sat there in silence, too shy to pray out loud. It is only recently that I have come to see that perhaps that is where my love of silence and the sense of God in it first began. My thoughts wandered as they do with most people, but I learned to sit still and wait on God and occasionally felt compelled to pray aloud.

My parents wanted me to become a teacher and would later find it very hard to let me go in order to train for ministry in the Anglican Church. It seemed to them that I was throwing away other opportunities besides rejecting things that they valued and my mother in particular felt alienated by the Church of England. Converted in her teens during the Second World War, the Baptist church was the only tradition she understood. My father on the other hand had been brought up in a village church, pumping the organ for a penny a week as a boy. He came to my confirmation and to my surprise quoted large chunks of the BCP. By then he was showing signs of dementia and I have experienced this rootedness in the Prayer Book liturgy in older people many times since. In a small way it encouraged me to think that the struggle involved in dealing with my family's misgivings concerning ordination was not terminal.

Growing up in the Baptist church involved attending Sunday School which was invariably taught by women. Two in particular had a huge impact on me and were role models of what lively and keen Christians should be like. They were fun as well as confident and committed in their faith. Another much older woman taught a Bible class and it was her faithfulness week in week out that left an impression on me. Sundays were for church and a great emphasis was placed on teaching the Bible. It was always a man of course but I loved to sit and listen to scripture expounded, forty minutes in the morning and forty minutes in the evening, every Sunday. It never occurred to me as the gray-suited deacons sat in a straight row at communion why it was OK that we had two female missionaries in the field teaching the Bible (and in one case physically helping to build the church), but at home they were not permitted to do so beyond the Sunday School.

In my second year I was asked if I would consider becoming CU rep for my college. This was the first instance of being asked to do something that I would never have considered myself and it has been something of a pattern in my life. It may be that the only way to get me to hear God's call is to make it loud and clear through someone else. This first request came out of the blue but I knew that I had to say yes. I took it very seriously and along with the other college rep prayed for and sought to encourage the other Christians in college. We wrote a CU letter at the end of each term and I discovered a love of writing these brief but constructive letters of encouragement and exhortation. We had a university-wide mission led by Michael Griffiths and it was a huge privilege to be involved in its planning and execution. Gradually I was discovering Christians from other churches who spoke about Jesus in the same terms that I used and clearly loved God. Some of them were Anglicans. One was a Roman Catholic. I am ashamed to say that initially I was astonished! I began to attend St Nicholas' church in the marketplace in Durham while George Carey was vicar and loved the worship in this warm and inviting church. It was of course a modern liturgy but that made it accessible to a Baptist encountering it for the first time.

I stayed in Durham following graduation and continued to discover more about the Christian faith beyond my small horizons. I embarked on a PhD in history which focused on the Reformation in England.

I was especially fascinated to discover the influence of women in the royal household where the new ideas about the Bible were concerned. It was impossible to ignore the theological issues among the historical and I was eager to set the Reformers in a wider context. I had a friend who introduced me to some medieval writers and I began reading some of the Christian classics. These years were an exciting time of discovery for me. I remember scouring the SPCK bookshop for devotional books and early coming across one called *Hungry for God* by Ralph Martin. It seemed to sum up my own desire to grow in Christ at that time.

One of the most significant turns in my road to ordination came when a fellow PhD student suggested that I apply to St John's College in Durham as a personal tutor. Ruth Etchells was the principal at that time and of course I had no idea that her appointment was such a ground-breaking event as she was a lay woman in charge of an Anglican theological college. (St John's incorporated Cranmer Hall as well as the undergraduate college.) The four years spent as a personal tutor were deeply formative. It was as though a number of things came together to form a clearer picture. I was studying the Reformation, the origins of the Book of Common Prayer and the sixteenth century roots of the Anglican Church. Thomas Cranmer was a key player in the politics of the Tudor court and royal household which was the focus of my research. I began to attend the daily office in the college chapel along with the ordinands in training and as with so many 'converts' to Anglicanism felt as though I had come home. It was the Alternative Service Book of course but it was the regularity, the repetition of the psalms and consistent intercession that drew me in and nourished my spirituality in new ways. I also met men and more significantly women who were training for full-time ministry. As I heard their stories and learned about the roles they were preparing for I felt for the first time that perhaps here was something that I could fit into too. Here were people studying theology, wrestling with faith and following a vocation. Inevitably I learned a new vocabulary and joined in conversations that stretched and challenged me. There was a lot of laughter too. I remember Michael Vasey and Peter Adam at breakfast one day challenging my notions of what made an evangelical and not getting the answer they were looking for. I had a lot to learn! In Ruth Etchells I found a wise counsellor who listened to my growing sense of calling to ordained ministry. I loved the pastoral work involved in having responsibility for a number of undergraduates and I loved taking my turn in giving out the wine at communion. There wasn't really a better place for making a gentle transition to the Anglican fold and I was duly confirmed just in time for my (as it was then) Advisory Council for the Church's Ministry.

I was told by my selectors that I need to broaden my experience of the Anglican Church, so for six months I worshipped at St Olave's church in York as I was living there for a while before commencing training at Ridley Hall in Cambridge. St Olave's was in the Anglo-Catholic tradition but it had an excellent relationship with St Michael le Belfrey just a few hundred yards away. One evening they had a joint service and the vicar of St Olave's commented that out of all the things they had in common the most important was the Holy Spirit. It was an important lesson for me and it took away any sense of nervousness I might feel around Christians who worshipped in different ways from those I was used to. I learned a lot from the quiet and dignified way worship was conducted in that church.

So ten years on I finally began my degree in theology and I didn't lose my faith or find it watered down and compromised. The theology faculty in

Cambridge valued its ordinands and I was blessed with tutors in both Old and New Testaments who asked me what implications I drew pastorally from the essay I had just written. They made me think and I was grateful that I had not done theology first time round so as to have the opportunity now and in such circumstances as ordination training afforded. I had witnessed the benefits of residential training in Durham and I was pleased to have the experience myself for three years. I remain convinced that residential training is still a very important component of how the Church of England prepares men and women for ordination in the twenty-first century. I needed the companionship of others to train alongside in order for the necessary spiritual formation to have a chance to happen. There were 52 of us when I started at Ridley Hall and only one other of these was a woman. That was in the late 1980s when only Cranmer Hall had a significant cohort of women among its ordinands. The numbers began to creep upwards while I was there, but the Baptist church meant I was used to seeing men leading and preaching in church with women in the background doing jobs behind the scenes and making up the numbers at the church meetings. In 1987, at the end of my first year, women were ordained deacon for the first time. Vivian Faull came to preach in the college chapel and she was the first woman with any leading position in the church that I had really encountered. I had been exposed to women preachers in Durham of course but they were licensed lay workers, even if they were on the staff at Cranmer Hall. This was different and I was part of the change.

I think I had a fairly easy journey with regards to being a woman from the time of answering God's call to ordination to well beyond the point of ordination. Throughout my training and curacy I was in a distinct minority, but I was used to that. The Church as I knew it was run by men, and women remained in the background. I was the only female curate in my Deanery and most of my fellow curates on the Post Ordination Training course (as it was then) were men as well. My Baptist friends did not understand why on earth I would want to be ordained and since there was suspicion around the Church of England anyway it simply increased their sense that I had somehow sold out to a liberal way of thinking. In many ways this was reassuring as I knew that this was more about prejudice than informed thinking, yet the little parrot that sat on my shoulder and told me I wasn't as sound as I used to be was never quite silenced. I did a lot of thinking and reading as an ordinand, going over and over the same Biblical texts and checking and re-checking my motives for seeking ordination. I knew God was calling me and had that call confirmed repeatedly by people I trusted and respected, but I could still hear the parrot. During my curacy I experienced little but good will. There was plenty of curiosity because most people had not encountered women with dog collars on before. I overheard an old farmer at the end of a funeral I had taken say firmly that he wasn't going to be buried by a woman, but for the most part, people were more likely to ask for the woman curate, especially for weddings and baptisms. I had so many opportunities to share the Gospel because people wanted to know why I had chosen this path.

Having this positive experience of practical ministry during my curacy confirmed and strengthened my convictions about women in leadership in the Church and the importance of the ordained ministry in this. Nevertheless, as I was ordained in 1989 it was expected that I would remain as a deacon for the foreseeable future. I didn't really concern myself with campaigning for the priesthood or stop to contemplate what difference that might make at this stage. I was having a great time as a curate anyway and I think my non-conformist roots meant that the importance of presiding at the Eucharist was not really central. Beside, my training incumbent was totally unthreatened by having a female curate and let me do everything I could possibly do as a deacon. I had an excellent training except for one thing and that was that I was not prepared in any way to become an incumbent. Why would I be? It was only when the diocese offered me a post that would have put me in charge of a parish that I realised how ill prepared I was to take it on. I was good at being second-in-command but terrified at the thought of being in charge myself. In looking back I think I panicked and at the first sign of hostility when exploring the possibility I gave up. Then when a one year post teaching Church history at Cranmer Hall came up I jumped at it, let off the hook, for the time being at least. That one year became three during which the measure for priesting women went through General Synod. I stood outside in Dean's Yard as the announcement was made (typically I was in London for something else and just happened to go along with a friend). I knew that things would never be the same for me as well as for everyone else and just wanted to be back in a parish.

I was priested in Durham Cathedral by David Jenkins as one of the 'Thirty Nine Articles' (there were thirty nine women ordained in 1994). The following year I was licensed as priest-in-charge of Cherry Burton and appointed as chaplain to Bishop Burton Agricultural College and Archbishop's Adviser in Rural Affairs. Having grown up in the countryside and having had experience of students the combination made a lot of sense. I found that having three separate areas of responsibility quite difficult, however, and less harmonious than I would have liked. In particular I found that chaplaincy was not my thing, especially as the traditional idea of a chaplain with a ministry of 'being there' was increasingly giving way to a model involving working in the student services department. I had no training for either model and as with so much of ministry, I had to rely on what I had observed in the past. The Rural Adviser's post was only for one day per week but it deepened in me a lasting commitment to rural churches.

It was the parish that energised and inspired me, even though I had not received much preparation for this either. About a year in as priest-in-charge I attended a diocesan training event for new incumbents, but at first I relied on ringing up friends who were incumbents to ask what to do in various situations in which I found myself. I had two female church wardens at Cherry Burton, one of whom was well up on faculty forms so that was one area at least I did not need to worry about. For the next five and a half years I came to forget that I was a woman priest. I was simply the priest in that place doing a job I enjoyed. I discovered, however, that being an incumbent can be very lonely at times and it took a lot of effort to maintain friendships outside the circle of the church.

While I was training I had a spiritual director from what was then the Institute of the Blessed Virgin Mary (now Companions of Jesus). Sister Pia offered a course on spiritual direction with her friend Imogen Ecclestone who was a therapist. This was a life changing experience for me. I had my first spiritual director in Durham and have had one ever since and have been involved in offering this ministry for almost thirty years. I have found it life-giving both to offer and to receive and now teach it as part of the master's programme at Durham. It is a one-to-one ministry involving both parties listening primarily to the Holy Spirit and it provides a safe space to articulate what goes on in times of prayer and how all aspects of life connect with faith. Hearing myself talk about prayer brings insight and new perspectives on what it means to live in God's loving presence at all times and not just those moments when we are aware of him. I have carried this ministry with me wherever I have gone and it is core to the way I understand and respond to God's call. It was an aspect of ministry I wanted to develop and eventually suggested to the bishop that I should drop the Rural Adviser part of the job and become 'Spirituality Adviser' instead. This was agreed and I was able to work at this alongside the other roles with a great deal of freedom and initiative. Various quiet days were put on and I gathered a useful list of people who could offer spiritual direction that I drew on when I was approached by people seeking a director. It was a hugely satisfying task to match people up in this way. Later on I co-led a 'Spir-Dir' course with another woman priest in the diocese. This was modelled on a course first run in the Southwark diocese by Gordon Geoff which involved participants committing to a day a month over two years to train as directors. These days included worship and reflection, workshops on topics such as depression, guilt, dreams and the arts as well as speakers coming to share various aspects of spiritual direction with the group. The Southwark courses spawned other courses around the country as people moved and set them up. I had done one myself in Newcastle while teaching at Cranmer Hall. We did the course twice and each time had a full quota of twenty participants who grew in faith and confidence in their time together. As far as I know those courses are still running and enabling people to accompany others in prayer.

Towards the end of my time at Cherry Burton I met and married another priest in rural ministry in the diocese. As I was over forty by now I was not expecting to get married at all. There were few people my own age in the parish, no Christian single men that I knew of and I was well aware that some men found women in dog collars off-putting anyway. But God surprised me. We were fifty miles apart so clearly one of us had to move. I felt less rooted than my husband at that point and we decided I would move to his part of the diocese. When I left my parish a woman who only attended church on special occasions brought her little girl to my farewell and afterwards thanked me for showing her daughter a model of a woman priest. I treasure that parting gift greatly because I am convinced that the best advocate of women's ministry is women simply doing the job in a transparent and unapologetic way.

There were a number of vacancies in my husband's area and I hoped that something would materialise, but it was not to be. I was told that I couldn't expect the diocese to find me a job and 'women usually expected to move with their husband's work.' Although I had just got married I found myself entering a very dark place. Overnight I went from being the rector of my own parish to being my husband's non-stipendiary assistant curate. I lost my stipend but it was not so much the loss of money but the loss of status that I struggled with. It felt as though I had fallen into a void and it certainly became a spiritual wilderness. Thirteen months later I gave birth to a son and with hindsight I think that God was making sure I did not try to be super-mum and super-vicar at the same time. I would, I suspect, have tried to show that being a full-time mother and a full-time incumbent were two compatible roles. Others since have found creative ways of combining these two roles but I do not think it is easy. I was able to enjoy being a new mother and still able to preach and preside, at least while my son was in his carry-cot. Life became more difficult once he was crawling and walking in country churches that were not used to small children being present.

Having a baby revolutionised my life beyond anything I had hitherto experienced. I had read Margaret Hebblethwaite's *Motherhood and God* years ago and found it very moving but now it took on a whole new realism for me. Not having had a conversion experience I think becoming a mother was the closest thing to it for me. It led me to re-think almost all my theology and I began to understand the relationship of God with us in new and deeply moving ways. Theological lights went on at every turn in my mind and engaged my heart and I found the early years of motherhood exhilarating. It transformed the spiritual wilderness and became a lifeline of hope and fresh possibility. The mothering of God with all it implies for loving and letting go continues to challenge me as I watch my son stretch his wings, test the world around and grow as a person.

For the first five years of motherhood I had to be content with whatever ministry came my way. With eight churches for my husband to look after there was always something to do in the parish and I valued presiding on a regular basis. I continued to offer spiritual direction and ran the courses mentioned earlier. I had already begun writing a weekly column on spirituality for the Church of England Newspaper and this became a regular spiritual discipline which continues to keep me grounded as I reflect on the Scriptures and write. I also began teaching spirituality two days a week back at Cranmer Hall. I had my mother nearby who was becoming increasingly frail but was always delighted to see her grandson as much as possible. I had no idea that all this was preparing me for the next stage of ministry that was to come my way.

Just as I was not looking for ordination at the time, nor was I looking for marriage when it surprised me, so I was not looking for a full-time job when it appeared. I opened the Church of England newspaper to see the post of 'Tutor in prayer spirituality and mission' at Wycliffe Hall in Oxford. My husband persuaded me to apply and I was offered the post. It was my dream job. It involved spiritual formation with ordinands, teaching spirituality (and a number of other things as I soon discovered) and being part of a community with a clear purpose. I do not think I have ever worked so hard and intensely in my life but it is work that I believe in and enjoy. Preparing men and women for the long haul of ministry is my motivating passion and as long as I keep that at the centre of vision I am energised for the task. Of course as with nearly all jobs, there are a lot of other things that seem to get in the way of the core task. Teaching in a theological college is no exception. For me it is important to stay grounded in practical life and ministry. Home life with family helps enormously with that, as does regularly preaching and presiding in a local rural parish. I teach theological reflection and discovered something I had been doing all my life! One of my teaching passions is to help evangelicals to do this better so as to make clear and theologically grounded connections between doctrine and everyday life. It is a challenge to demystify something that every Christian can and should do all the time.

Currently I am Dean of Women at Wycliffe and am trying to promote the college as a positive place for women to train. It is ironic that until I came to Oxford I had never needed to campaign on behalf of women among other evangelicals. Others had paved the way to make it possible for me. Among the many comments I had grown used to hearing were those from male clergy who remarked how much better the advent of women's ordination had made the priesthood in general. Whether we argue that women are equal but different or maintain that we are all the same, there is no doubt in my mind that the leaders of the body of Christ need to be representative of both genders. Not all evangelicals share that view and I have been saddened to find myself having to be so pro-active in a context where the numbers of women training to be leaders has diminished so significantly in recent years. I am acutely aware that this is true of the wider context of evangelicalism, especially among young women. Why are they not coming forward to train for ordained ministry? The women I have trained for leadership in the last five and a half years have been outstanding: gifted, creative, inspiring and clearly called by God. They are now scattered around both here and abroad in all kinds of ministries and hearing from different ones from time to time is a joy and a confirmation that women are called. I would love to see more women, especially young women becoming Bible teachers, theologians and church leaders so that the body of Christ may flourish as God intends.

At Wycliffe I teach a number of subjects: spirituality, worship and theological reflection in particular and I am responsible for three weeks of integrated studies. I especially enjoy putting together these integrated weeks where students engage with a subject in a multi-faceted way. So for example we have a course on death and bereavement which involves thinking about the Christian understanding of death, the theological issues around death, dying and bereavement, we look at what the Bible says about these areas and we think through how to offer pastoral care of those who are dying and those bereaved. We visit a local funeral home and the crematorium and each student prepares and delivers a sermon for a fictional situation. This to me is where theology comes to life as we work hard at Scripture and doctrine but also at the numerous different contexts into which we expect God to speak. Sometimes it is important to say that women's experience is different and this enlarges our horizons further and enables the Church to include rather than exclude.

I approach the teaching of spirituality from both a historical perspective and a contemporary one. The historian in me is fascinated by how Christians in a different age and different circumstances: the desert Fathers and Mothers, the early Celtic and Anglo-Saxon Christians in the British Isles, the Reformers of the sixteenth century or the evangelical revival movement have lived out the Christian faith. In what ways do they continue to teach, challenge and encourage us in our own discipleship today? Coming to the present what is the contemporary interest in spirituality outside the churches about and how may we bridge the interest with the Gospel? What does it mean to develop a Christian spirituality in today's world? These are important questions for men and women to think through as they train for ministry.

Much as I love reading and teaching I also want to be out there practising and I take a monthly service for a small congregation nearby each month and continue to have a small number of people who come for spiritual direction. These aspects of life keep me grounded and fresh and cause me to ask questions that send me back to the Bible and to prayer.

One of the biggest challenges is juggling home life with work. Both could easily be all-consuming and it is easy to slip into guilt in either sphere, but especially where home is concerned. Trying to be a good wife and mother as well as working hard and going the extra mile at work does not always work. There are some strategies that help, especially planning ahead and making sure time with my husband and son are also planned into the diary alongside other commitments. It continues to be a learning experience and I am pleased to learn from others who have also grappled with these issues. Juggling work and family brings big challenges for women but I have encountered women who do it well and with grace as well as panache. It is an exciting time to be a Christian woman in ministry and I am pleased to be a part of it.

One voice surrounded by many

Kate Wharton

In my ministry as Priest in Charge of St George's Church in Everton, Liverpool, I find myself constantly feeling astonished and thinking "how on earth did this happen?!" I'm astonished because never in a million years would I have thought that this is what I would end up doing. And I'm astonished too because it just feels so 'right', so completely 'me' – I know that I'm doing the very thing that I was created to do.

I'm still not entirely sure how it did happen. As a child, church was very important to me. I was an only child and, when we moved from London to Southport shortly before my third birthday, my parents began sending me to Sunday School so that I'd meet some other children. We lived just down the road from the church and Sunday School was great fun (church was less so...!). At that time my parents themselves didn't go to church, although they do now. I stayed in Sunday School throughout my whole childhood, and was also in Brownies and Guides. At the age of 12 I made a decision for myself to become a Christian, and was confirmed (having been baptised a month earlier, still recovering from the horror of discovering that my parents hadn't had me baptised as a baby!). I stayed on at church after lots of my friends left because it wasn't cool any more! I was a server, a Sunday School helper, and a bell ringer. Church was part of my life, and yet it was just one part along with many others, and there was certainly never any thought of future ministry.

I was 14 when the vote went through General Synod to allow women to be priests. I do remember it, but only in a fairly abstract way, as some 'out there' item of news which seemed generally to be a good thing, but which didn't have much bearing on my day to day life. It hadn't ever occurred to me to wonder whether or not I was 'in favour' of women getting ordained – I mean, of course I was, how could there be any other point of view, and how come it had taken so long?! I certainly wasn't aware at the time of the significance of the fact that women were being approved to become priests, but not bishops.

My main concerns at that time were those of any teenage girl – spending time with friends, wondering what boys were all about, trying to pass my GCSEs, and working out what to do with the rest of my life. I spent some time trying to decide between physiotherapy and speech and language therapy and eventually, after a fantastic gap year in Borneo, went to Leeds Metropolitan University to train to become a Speech and Language Therapist. On arriving in Leeds as a very naïve and not-very-discipled young Christian, I joined the Christian Union, and on my first Sunday, took myself off to the local Church of England church, expecting something similar to my familiar middle-of-the-road church from home. To my surprise I discovered instead a vibrant, lively, evangelical church with hundreds of people, many of whom were my own age. Up until this point I hadn't encountered many Christians under the age of 50 so this was something of a shock! It was completely alien and from the very first moment of walking through the door, I loved it! It's no exaggeration to say that I immediately felt that I had come home.

My faith grew in huge leaps and bounds over the next few years. I got involved with the student work at church, and started to attend the church plant, which met on a nearby housing estate. I would go there in the morning and to the 'big church' in the evening. I was also very involved with the Christian Union at Uni. It was a fantastic time in my life. I loved my course, I loved being a student, and I loved church. I thought that I'd discovered the thing which I wanted to spend the rest of my life doing. In fact, I had discovered it – but it wasn't the thing that I thought it was.

During my final year at university, happily training for my future career, I suddenly and very unexpectedly found myself feeling called to get ordained. It was very clear that this was a call from God because it was a million miles from the plan that I had for my life! There was a moment at which I first became aware of this sense of calling, and I can still remember it vividly, but there were lots of other important moments too, lots of points at which God spoke very clearly. He needed to speak clearly, and He needed to do so over and over again because I was really not impressed at what it was that I could hear Him saying!

There were many, many reasons in my mind as to why I couldn't possibly be a vicar. All of the vicars I'd known before going to my current church had been old men. Although I did now know some younger vicars, and even some female ones, it still definitely didn't seem like something that a 21 year old woman could be seriously considering as a future career path. The 15 years of my life which had been spent in a more traditional church seemed to have more influence over my brain at this time than the 3 in an evangelical church, since when I thought about what exactly it was that vicars did, I had images of singing evensong in draughty old buildings, going to bring and buy sales, and wearing odd clothes. I hope it doesn't sound disrespectful if I say that my image of the ordained ministry at that point was fairly grey, drab and dull. It was in no way an appealing prospect! Plus, my singing voice is terrible!

Unfortunately, despite all my efforts to pretend that this wasn't happening, the fact was that it most definitely was. Before then I couldn't have told you what it felt like to be 'called by God' to do something; but at the time I was completely sure that this was it. It was a nagging feeling that would never go away, but was there, just under the surface, all the time. It was a sense of uncertainty every time I thought about the future, unless I thought about a vicaring future, in which case all felt calm and peaceful. It was several people, some I knew and some I didn't, telling me that they had a funny feeling, or they'd had a dream, and they wondered about me possibly getting ordained – did that sound crazy? It was an ever more bizarre collection of signs and hints and pictures everywhere I went – from posters on church doors to bumping into vicars in the street. It was that pit-of-the-stomach feeling of rightness whenever I thought about it – crazy as it continued to seem to me.

At the same time as wrestling with it all, I was finishing my degree, graduating, and getting my first job as a Speech and Language Therapist. I absolutely loved my job, which didn't exactly help with the discernment process! Throughout that year I continued to pray and wonder and argue with God. Eventually I decided to test things further by working for the church, so I gave up my wonderful job and became a pastoral assistant, based at the church plant. Of course I loved that too! It was different though – it wasn't just a job that I enjoyed, it was 'me'. It felt so totally right that I never looked back. I went through all the selection procedures and the following September found myself training at Wycliffe Hall in Oxford.

The year that I spent working for the church was especially formative for me in terms of my calling. Not only was I working with a fantastic team of people, I was also living and working in the midst of a fantastic community. This was my first experience of urban ministry and I loved it. The estate experienced all of the social problems that you might expect in that sort of area, and life was often tough, but my overriding memories are of a loving, caring, friendly, fun, welcoming community. When I went to college I went knowing that my call to ordained ministry was tied in with a call to urban ministry—for me, the two are inseparable.

People have often asked me in the years since then how and why I decided to become a vicar. That's nearly always the word they use – 'decided'. I find it a really hard question to answer, partly because the whole issue of calling is a really tricky one to explain, but mainly because to be perfectly honest it never did feel like a decision. It was, rather, something that I simply couldn't help but do. It wasn't something that I chose, or even something that I particularly wanted to do (although I had managed to get over my fear of being made to sing evensong for eternity). I had absolutely no idea why God would want to call me to do this job (to be honest, I still haven't). And yet, at the same time, I was completely certain that He was calling me to do it. Really all that happened was that I came to understand that there was no point ignoring this, because it wasn't going to go away. There was a huge amount of liberation in this because in the middle of one of my regular tantrums with God, when I shouted at Him that I didn't want to do this, and that it was too hard, and that I couldn't do it, He replied (not audibly, but nevertheless quite clearly) that He was well aware that I couldn't do it, but that He could, and that all I had to do was allow Him to do that. The 'Awesome verse' was what got me through this time – in The Message, 2 Corinthians 12:9 reads like this – "My grace is enough; it's all you need. My strength comes into its own in your weakness." (MSG) In the end, that was what I came to accept and understand – that all I had was my weakness, but that that was all I needed, because God's grace was enough.

I absolutely loved the three years I spent training at Wycliffe Hall in Oxford. It was a bit of a shock to the system being a student again, but at least I hadn't been away from studying for very long, so I could remember how to write essays! It felt like such a privilege to be able to spend every day studying the Bible and preparing to work in church. It was hard work, but it was almost always fun, and the friends I made during that time are still the closest friends I have.

When the time came to look for a curacy I wanted to be as open as I could be to different possibilities; however I had come to realise that for me there were two non-negotiables in terms of my future ministry. One was that I would now happily and certainly place myself within the 'charismatic evangelical' box in terms of my theology and practice; the other was that I felt very clearly called to minister in what the Church of England has tended to call 'Urban Priority Areas'. These two clear criteria meant that, at that time, I couldn't find a curacy in Ripon and Leeds Diocese from where I had come, and so I was on my own as I looked for my first post. I wrote to every Diocese in 'the north', and among the first responses was one from Liverpool. Since this was the Diocese in which I had grown up, and where my parents still lived, I looked there first.

I spent a weekend with Sam Nicholson, the vicar of St Luke's Church, and her husband Jim, and their two lovely children. When I arrived, very late after getting horribly lost, and was greeted with a Chinese takeaway and a glass of wine, I felt that I might very well have found somewhere where I could happily spend the next four years! After a great weekend walking round the parish and attending the church, Sam and I were both agreed that this was the right place for me to spend my curacy (it may have helped that I wasn't fazed at the sight of a burnt out double-decker bus as we turned a corner. Sam exclaimed in surprise, "gosh, that wasn't there yesterday!"). I was ordained Deacon at Liverpool Cathedral on 25th June 2005, and Priest the following year. I spent just under four years at St Luke's and learnt a huge amount, especially in the final year, as Sam had left so I was able to practise being a real vicar!

A vacancy for an incumbent came up at St George's Church in Everton as I was nearing the end of my curacy and it seemed to be a perfect fit. I was appointed as Priest in Charge and was licensed in March 2009. I've recently celebrated my fourth anniversary there, and it's been a fantastic four years. I do still have to pinch myself on an almost daily basis to confirm that it's true; I have somehow been allowed to become a real live vicar. I often wonder whether they've noticed that I don't in fact have the first clue about what I'm doing most of the time. At the same time, however, I couldn't be happier than doing the job I'm currently doing, and I couldn't be more sure that this is the right path for my life, the thing which God created me to do. I imagine that I'll probably spend the rest of my ordained life thinking that I don't have a clue what I'm doing – and that's quite possibly as it should be, because it reminds me to keep relying on God all the time! One of my favourite Bible verses in recent years has been 1 Thessalonians 5:24, and I have it written on the door to my study to remind myself that God has called me to this work, and that, ultimately (thank goodness!)

He is in charge – "The one who calls you is faithful and He will do it."

Often people ask me whether I've ever experienced any difficulties as an ordained woman, but to be honest I really haven't. At college there were obviously people who disagreed with the ordination of women but the vast majority of them were nevertheless kind and supportive, and the staff dealt quickly and well with any issues which did arise. The Diocese of Liverpool is a wonderfully affirming and positive place to work as a woman. Happily, I can count on one hand the number of negative comments I've received in eight years of ordained ministry.

Interestingly, people seem to be far more likely to comment on my age than my gender, and their comments are almost exclusively positive. I went to college at 24, was ordained at 27, and became an incumbent at 30, so I guess I am a fair bit younger than people expect! Also I wonder whether the combination of age and gender together provoke even more comments.

The people of Liverpool are warm, generous and very funny. I've been called a 'dolly bird' at a funeral visit (meant in a nice way, I think!), and people often tell me how great it is to see a young woman priest. In fact, I've begun to worry about the point at which they'll stop calling me young (although given most people's stereotypes about church and clergy I'll probably be ok for a couple of decades yet!) In the first week of my curacy, walking to church wearing a pink clerical shirt, I was greeted cheerily with, "Morning Father!" People often ask "so what do we call you then love?" to which I tend to reply "well I'll answer to most things, but Kate will do for a start!"

I absolutely love my ministry at St George's. I've been warmly welcomed into the community and have enjoyed getting to know people. Everton is a deprived urban area in many ways with lots of the social problems and issues which you might expect – high unemployment, high crime, poverty, anti-social behaviour and more. But these words don't begin to describe it. People are kind and welcoming and caring. They want their lives, and the lives of the children who will come after them, to be better.

In Liverpool, in contrast with some other parts of the UK, church still has a big role to play in society and in most people's lives. People respect church and Christianity and what they stand for, even if they don't always realise what vibrant, relevant, active Jesus-following can look like today.

People appreciate the fact that I've come to live in Everton and have chosen to be part of their community. Although mostly they're happy living there, people are not naive – they recognise the issues which exist in the community. Sometimes they ask why I'm here, as if they think perhaps I've been sent here as a punishment! When I say that I chose to come and live here, and that I'm in it for the long haul, they're sometimes surprised, but they're always pleased. In communities like this one, people come and go a lot. Whether it's GPs, police or teachers, professionals 'drop in and do good' for a little while but then quickly move on. And even when they're 'here' often they aren't really here – they may work in the community but then they drive out to their nice homes each evening. As a vicar, it's important to me that I'm really present here, really part of the community. It speaks volumes about our incarnate God, who chose to come and live among us. And when people deal drugs in my garden, and throw bricks through my window, I identify all the more with people who sometimes love living here, and sometimes find it hard, but simply call it home.

As vicar of a small, poor church, where the 'staff team' consists of just me, it's possible to end up feeling like a Jack of all trades. I have to get stuck in to most things, whether or not I'd consider them to be my gifts or my preferences. I'm in the process of building up a team of leaders to work alongside me, but until then I'll have to continue to try my hand at whatever comes along. At the same, however, there are some things which will always make my heart beat faster!

In terms of ordained ministry, as I said earlier, my call was tied up with a call to urban areas, and (as much as we can ever predict the future!) that's where I see myself continuing to live and work. I want, like Jeremiah, to continue to "seek the peace and prosperity of the city." (Jeremiah 29:7) It breaks my heart (because I believe it breaks God's) when people live in material and spiritual poverty, when they have no aspirations for the future because they can't see how things could ever change, when they believe they're worthless because that's all they've ever been told, when they settle for less than the full life which they're offered in Jesus.

Sometimes it can feel pretty hard to live and work in one of the most deprived parts of the country. I often find myself recalling that for a brief period as a student I thought about going overseas to do long term mission work. That turned out not to be God's plan for me, but I do sometimes feel quite a lot like a cross-cultural missionary. The culture in which I live and work is not 'my' culture, any more than if I lived and worked in India or Uganda it would not be 'my' culture. That doesn't mean that I don't feel called to be here, and it doesn't mean that I don't love it (most of the time!). It does mean, however, that it can sometimes feel pretty exhausting just to live here, even before I do anything else.

Having said that, if was offered the chance to leave here tomorrow and go and work somewhere more 'familiar' culturally, I wouldn't go. I am here because I know this is God's place for me at this time. I am absolutely certain that God has called me to be a vicar, and He's called me, for now, to work in Everton, and so I do it with enthusiasm because I want nothing more than to be obedient to Him.

My primary gift is as a teacher, and I love nothing more than to preach about God's love, telling people how amazingly fabulous God thinks they are, and about the offer of eternal life which is theirs through Jesus. My greatest joy is to witness that moment when people 'get it'—when they first understand that it really is true, not just for everyone else but for them too. I love to see people realise that God really did create them, that Jesus really did die for them, that the Holy Spirit really is active in the world—that the gospel really is true.

I think, on reflection, that all of the things about

which I'm most passionate come back to the same basic starting point – helping those who have been marginalised, for whatever reason, to discover their immense value and worth to God. It's so easy, I think, for us to undersell God's emotions. I believe that God gets angrier than we sometimes give Him credit for, and I believe He feels compassion infinitely more than we can ever understand or imagine. I think God really, really hates injustice. I think He hates it when people are made to feel that they don't matter, or that others are more important than they are, or that they have nothing to offer. Our hearts should also break for these things which break God's heart.

That's why I love working in deprived inner city areas—with, for and amongst poor people.

Many of them have been told, maybe explicitly by those in authority, or maybe implicitly by policies and practices in society, that they don't matter quite as much as those living in the 'better' parts of the country. People in our most deprived areas often feel as though they are ignored, over and over again, by the people with power and influence. I want them to realise, to truly understand and believe, that God is for them, that He's on their side, that they matter to Him, and that He is interested in their lives.

It's also why I love working with and among

people with disabilities. We live in a world which strives for perfection in terms of appearance and ability. Those who don't look quite the same as others, or can't do certain things, or have an impairment of some sort, are often treated as if they have less value than other people. When people with any sort of disability are discriminated against, ignored or undervalued I don't just think God gets upset, I think He gets angry. How dare we tell anyone who has been made in God's image that they don't matter? How dare we imply that some people have less worth than others because there are certain things that they aren't able to do?

For eight years I volunteered at the New Wine summer conference with 'Our Place', the ministry seeking to support children, young people and adults with additional needs, and their families, in order that they could fully access all the activities available there. It was always one of the main highlights of my year. We would work with approximately 100 families, enabling them to enjoy a relaxing holiday, perhaps for the first time ever, as they were supported and cared for. I've also been involved with training events for local churches, helping them to work out how best to value and include everyone of all needs and abilities.

Within Liverpool Diocese I was also for eight years part of the ministry team working among deaf people (although I have recently stepped back from this as I've become Area Dean). I'm proud of the fact that the week after I was ordained priest I presided twice in two different languages—at my curacy church in the morning in English, and at the Deaf church in the afternoon, in British Sign Language!

I passionately believe that our churches should be fully open and accessible to anyone and everyone, and that it's our responsibility to ensure everyone is able to hear and understand the good news in a way which is appropriate to them.

I think that this desire to see marginalised people fully welcomed and included also in some way describes my final great passion within ministry, although it might not be as immediately obvious as the other two!

A few years ago I was asked to speak at New Wine on the subject of singleness. Now, I am indeed single, so I was more qualified than some of the people I've heard speak on the subject, but I wasn't at all sure that it was something I wanted to do. At first I said no, but later I woke up one morning with two titles in my head, and a clear sense that I needed to do two talks, one for each of those titles. This was fairly unexpected, but I went ahead and began to plan the two talks. To my great surprise I really enjoyed both planning and delivering them. People seemed to appreciate what I said, perhaps most particularly the honesty with which I tried to tackle the whole area. I began to be invited to more and more places to speak on this subject. The very last thing I'd envisaged was that I'd become some sort of 'singleness expert', but that's what seemed to be happening, at least in other people's minds! And as it happened, I found a growing passion for the topic. I longed for single people to live the 'life to the full' that we see promised in John's gospel, rather than putting their life on hold for some possible future marriage.

And the marginalisation that I mentioned? Well, I think that very often single people are, or at least feel as though they are, treated in some way as second class citizens within many churches. This is far from being what the churches intend, of course, but nevertheless it is often what ends up happening. The more I've spoken publicly on this subject, and the more conversations I've had with single Christians right across the country from a whole variety of different churches, the more I've heard examples of what this looks like in practice. One of the two titles I first spoke on was this—"Living a God-obsessed life in a marriage-obsessed church." This might sound harsh, and perhaps it overstates the case to make a point, but the fact is that for many single Christians, that's what church feels like, and I believe it's something that churches really need to wake up to and take notice of if we're to avoid alienating single people and making them think that church has nothing to offer them.

The other title I first spoke on was "Living a God-obsessed life in a sex-obsessed world." I really do think that today in the west we live in a culture which is obsessed with sex. It's used to sell almost every product imaginable, on television, on billboards, and in magazines. Children have a terrifying amount of knowledge about things that a generation ago they wouldn't have even heard of. It seems that there are no longer any boundaries in this area. Nothing is unacceptable (apart from, perhaps, being a virgin past the age of 18!).

These two themes sum up why I think single people can sometimes feel like a marginalised group in our society today. We may feel marginalised in church because people don't know how to treat us, because everyone wants to see us married off, because we're seen as not quite 'grown up' yet, because we're not given the same responsibilities as those who are married, because 'family' themed events feel as though they exclude us. We may feel marginalised outside of church because people think we're odd if we choose to live celibate lives, because the lifestyle choices we make are not understood, because we're single in a different way from non-Christians—a way which is about purity and chastity rather than simply freedom to sleep around.

After I had done those first two talks, I found myself being asked to speak on this subject more and more. From being reluctant the first time, I became excited and passionate about it! I've now spoken at all of the New Wine summer conferences, and at various other churches and events. It certainly seems as though this is a topic which needs to be addressed at this moment. If I was surprised to find myself speaking on this topic, I was completely astonished to find myself writing a book on it! A friend had casually remarked one day that with all these talks I was now doing, I must have a few book chapters ready. I laughed, but the thought didn't go away, and before long I found myself sending three draft chapters to Monarch, and anxiously waiting for their response. They liked what they read, and in late 2012 I sent them the completed manuscript of my first book, Single Minded.

I mentioned earlier that feeling of not really

knowing what I'm doing, and wondering how on earth I've got to this point. I don't think that has ever been more true than with the publication of the book! As each stage has passed—sending in the draft chapters, being commissioned to write the whole book, finishing it only a week over deadline after a lot of late nights, getting the first proof copy, having my own book launch—I have grown more incredulous. How did this happen?! I am so thrilled that something I have written, something which is so close to my heart, is going to be read by (I hope!) many people, and (I really hope) make a difference to how single people live, and to how churches value and affirm and include single people.

People (especially other ordained friends) have asked me how on earth I found time to write a book, and how long it took, and what the secret is. The truth is that I'm not really sure! Like so many things in my life, I can't quite recall the moment at which I decided to do it. It was just yet another thing, along with getting ordained, and being called to work in deprived urban areas, and coming to St George's, which were just 'right'. I'm so grateful to God for the really clear ways in which He's spoken to me throughout my life, which have made it easy to do difficult things, because I've known for sure that He was in them all. I've got no idea what the future holds. At the time of writing I've just become Area Dean of Liverpool North Deanery, which will be an exciting new challenge alongside everything else! Where will I be in 5 years' time? I have no idea! What I pray, however, is that I'll still be following Jesus, going wherever He calls, doing whatever He asks, having fun, taking risks, living life to the full and continuing to know, every day, in the very core of my very being, His grace which is enough which is all I need.